Experiencing Authenticity

In A Shallow World

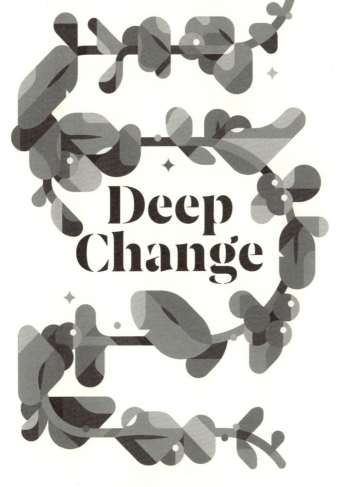

Deep Change

JASON ISAACS

Author of Toxic Soul

All rights reserved solely by the author. No part of this book can be reproduced in any form without permission from the author.

Unless otherwise indicated, Scripture quotations are taken from the Holy Bible, New Living Translation, copyright © 1996, 2004, 2007 by Tyndale House Foundation. Used by permission of Tyndale House Publishers Inc. Carol Stream, Illinois 60188. All Rights Reserved.

For more information, contact the author by email: jason@realhopenow.com

Copyright © 2022 Jason Isaacs/Daily Faith + Life

Deep Change: Experience Spiritual Depth In A Shallow World

Printed in China

To the elders of Hope City Church: Thank you for standing with me. It is a privilege to be your pastor.

Contents

Introduction - A Soul with Wings — 10

Part 1
Foundations

1. Defining Normal — 23
2. Why You Want What You Want — 34
3. Nothing to Prove — 48

Part 2
Practices

Practice #1 - Feel Your Feelings

4. Permission to Be Human — 57
5. There's a Word for That — 71
6. The Language of Prayer — 82

Practice #2 - Face Your Past

7. Looking Back to Move Forward — 94
8. Family of Origin — 106
9. The Story of Pain — 120

Practice #3 - Change Your Habits

10. The Overstimulated Soul — 132
11. Spiritual Disciplines — 143
12. Something More Beautiful — 161

Practice #4 - Embrace Your Limits

13. The Courage to Say No	174
14. Striding or Striving?	189
15. Easy Everywhere	202
Epilogue - Another Trip to Moriah	214
From the Author	219
Acknowledgments	220
Appendices	221
Notes	236

"The life we live out in our moments, hours, days, and years wells up from a hidden depth. What is in our 'heart' matters more than anything else for who we become and what becomes of us."
-Dallas Willard

"I am the vine, you are the branches. He who abides in Me, and I in him, bears much fruit..."
-Jesus

INTRODUCTION

A Soul with Wings

> "The box was broken for years, and yet it never occurred to anyone to buy another. The unspoken ethos of the men was always to manage with half-broken things or mend them. We called it 'making do.'"
> -**James Rebanks** *Pastoral Song*

One day, Jesus was approached and asked, "What is the most important commandment in the law?" This was a common conversation starter for first-century rabbis, teachers, and intellectuals. They were asking, "Based on your lifelong study and expertise, what do you think God cares about most?"

Jesus' answer was not controversial—he responded, "Love the Lord God with all your heart, soul, mind, and strength." He was quoting a verse from Deuteronomy that everyone listening would have been familiar with. But then He added a caveat: "And love your neighbor as yourself." This was unexpected. It wasn't a verse you could find in the Old Testament, nor was it a small tweak to Rabinnic teaching. By adding those five words, Jesus was confronting the religious tendency to compartmentalize our spiritual life and our everyday life.

According to Jesus, the Christian life is something that happens in your soul, mind, and body—the way you feel, think, and act—and as your relationship with Jesus changes your interior life, it changes your social life too. How you react on a random Tuesday morning with an annoying coworker says as much about your spiritual condition as the amount of church services you attend or Bible verses you read.

Jesus' answer is known as "The Greatest Commandment," but sadly it feels like "The Great Suggestion"—relegated to the hyperspiritual who have the time to dedicate themselves to "heavenly things." The rest of us desperately want to experience God in deeply personal ways, but it's just too impractical. We long for transcendence, but settle for busyness. In an age of progress, speed, and promotion, we struggle to value what we can't measure. Cultural influence has made it so bank accounts, square footage, and body mass index tend to inspire us much more than character development and spiritual formation.

But I believe the greatest obstacle to a "heart and soul" love for God is that for many, the commands of the Bible feel lofty and idealistic. What does it even mean to love God with all your heart, soul, mind, and strength, anyway? It's almost grandiose; the sort of thing that would be nice to achieve, but was really only within reach for a few heroic spiritual gurus who lived in the desert or sold all their possessions. Since we don't really know anyone we can clearly classify as "loving God with all their soul," we assume no one does, and Jesus meant it in some metaphorical way, like turning the other cheek. "Yes, love God the best you can," we think, "but don't be disappointed if you never achieve 'all your heart and soul' status."

The pages of scripture seem so far removed from our day-to-day life that we struggle to believe Jesus' teachings could ever make a practical difference. We've become disillusioned to the idea that our spirituality is tangible. Characteristics of the Christian life, like kindness to enemies, genuine humility, purity, and freedom from anger, anxiety, envy, or bitterness are aspirations, but we don't believe we could actually become those *kinds* of people. We feel our best hope is to try to be a slightly better version of who we've always been. But the core message of the Gospel is that God invades us with new life, and the setting for this new life is in the present—the carpool line, the gym, the cubicle, the waiting room, and the kitchen table.

We often tell ourselves, "nobody's perfect," and while this is true, we tend to say it in resignation because we feel inadequate comparing our reality to Jesus' possibility. It's easy to believe our failures are due to a lack of fervor or faith. Growing up in Bible-Belt Pentecostalism, I'm sensitive to the harmful idea that intensity is the best gauge for the quality of your spiritual life. This almost always leads to hypocrisy or shame when you can't seem to muster enough passion to stay as committed as you want to be.

Regardless of how hard you try, you will never be sinless, but it is possible to sin *less*. You will never be completely like Jesus, but it is possible to be *more* like Him. You may never be free of all fear, anxiety, or anger, but it is possible, through a relationship with Jesus and moment-by-moment interactions with the Holy Spirit, to become a much *less* angry, anxious, and fearful person. Loving God with all of your heart, soul, mind, and strength is possible!

This is not something only "special" Christians do; this is the invitation available to everyone who has placed their faith in the saving work of Jesus Christ. His spirit now lives in you, and has the power to transform you, from the inside out, into a completely new person. Unfortunately, because it feels too lofty or too vague, we place it on the shelf of unreasonable expectations and settle for an underwhelming version of Christianity that replaces soul transformation with behavior modification. We merge our religion with other religions and cultural self-help slogans and end up with a goal of being kind, successful, helpful, and measurable. Spiritual mastery becomes defined as being a "good" person.

C. S. Lewis said, "For mere improvement is not redemption, though redemption always improves people… God became man to turn creatures into sons: not simply to produce better men of the old kind but to produce a new kind of man. It is not like teaching a horse to jump better and better but like turning a horse into a winged creature."

A new *kind* of man or woman. Is that how you would describe your Christian experience? Do you feel like a new person? Do you feel like your soul grew wings? Do you feel that your old way of life has really "passed away?" Or, instead, would you say you're just trying to be a reasonably responsible person who limits your mistakes, and makes good choices as often as possible?

How many Christians do you know who have been radically transformed into a completely different person? Do you know someone who was incredibly self-righteous and legalistic but became more gracious? Someone who was addicted and gave up their dependencies? Someone who was extremely rude, impatient, critical, or lazy, but through a relationship with Jesus became a person of love, joy, peace, patience, kindness, and self-control? As a pastor of a congregation myself, I am often convicted by just how surprised we are when someone actually experiences a life-changing transformation. Sadly, for many churchgoers, the practical implications of their faith are "too trivial to be true."

In his book *The Spirit of the Disciplines*, Dallas Willard asks the question:

> "How can ordinary human beings such as you and I—who must live in circumstances all too commonplace—follow and become like Jesus Christ? How can we be like Christ always—not just on Sundays when we're on our best behavior, surrounded by others to cheer and sustain us? How can we be like him not as a pose or by a constant and grinding effort, but with the ease and power he had—flowing from the inner depths, acting with quiet force from the innermost mind and soul of the Christ who has become a real part of us? There is no question that we are called to this. It is our vocation as well as our greatest good. And it must be possible. But how?"

That is what this book is about.

How I Got Here

I've heard it said that to write a great book, you must first become the book. While this is not a book about me, a little backstory will help you understand why I'm so passionate about people experiencing deep change, and how I came to practice the lessons you will learn in the pages that follow.

I'm a fourth-generation preacher's kid, so it's not an exaggeration to say I've been in church my entire life. When I was 15, I surrendered my life to Jesus and began taking my faith seriously. After graduating high school, I married my wife, Andrea, and got into the family business, becoming a youth pastor at the age of 20. Over the next 17 years I had a few different jobs, but eventually became the senior pastor of Hope City Church, where I currently serve, in Louisville, Kentucky.

Due to my rich spiritual heritage, I jumped into pastoral ministry with relative ease. This is not to say I didn't have my struggles. My family dealt with some tragedies, and the church went through a few challenging seasons, but for the most part, every trouble in my life could be overcome with a little prayer, a pep talk, and determination. But then everything changed. Through a series of events that took me completely by surprise, I woke up one Friday morning overwhelmed by a paralyzing fear that I had never experienced before. I was certain that something awful was going to happen to me—maybe death, but hundreds of other options ran through my mind too. I had never considered myself a fearful person; I was always the guy who kept his cool when everyone else was freaking out! But over the next six months, I experienced panic attacks and severe episodes of fear. I would jump every time my phone would ring or the delivery man would drop off a package at the door. I would struggle to get out of bed or leave my house. I would sit in parking lots and wait for as many people to leave the store as possible before I walked in. There were some Sundays I would sit in the office and cry until my wife and a few of the elders came and helped me face the congregation to preach.

The worst moment was one weekday at church when I saw someone walking toward the front door. I couldn't see who it was, but I immediately panicked and assumed it was someone coming to hurt me, so I ran and hid in the sanctuary sound booth for 15 minutes, struggling to catch my breath, until I was sure they were gone. As I sat there against the wall of the booth I wondered, "How did you end up here?"

Life felt like a tidal wave of uncertainty and helplessness, and I couldn't figure out why this was happening or how it got this bad. I was a Christian. I read the Bible, faithfully attended church, and did my best to live a life that honored God. I was a pastor, for goodness' sake! But for the first time in my life, I felt like I had a problem that my faith could not fix. My spirituality never felt shallow before, but now I felt a mile wide and an inch deep. How could I have been a Christian for more than 20 years and not been acquainted with my fears, anxiety, sadness, and insecurities? My relationship with Jesus had never forced me to face the truth about what was happening beneath the surface of my life.

I wasn't losing my faith or doubting God; I was doubting myself. I had always thought I was a relatively healthy, spiritually mature person, but I was forced to take an inventory of my life, and I realized all my biblical knowledge and church attendance had done very little to develop my interior life. I didn't have the spiritual depth or the emotional health I thought I did. I had no awareness or language for what I was experiencing emotionally. I could not sit still and be alone in silence with God. I was oblivious to my need for approval and the way my insecurities drove me to project a certain lifestyle. I began to realize how much I had used my faith to attain the life I wanted instead of the life Jesus wanted for me.

I knew I had to do something, so I started by purchasing every book I could find that seemed as if it could help, and if those authors mentioned another author, I purchased those books too. I began reading authors like Eugene Peterson, Dallas Willard, Henri Nouwen, David G. Benner, John Mark Comer, and Peter Scazzero, just to name a few.* I read stories about early church mystics and the desert fathers. I read about liturgy and the monastic life, and I learned that for thousands of years, Christian leaders had been writing about spiritual formation—an invitation by God for contemplative living, spiritual depth, and emotional health. It's an invitation to leave the shallow brand of spirituality that has very little effect on my feelings, habits, bodily tendencies, and social interactions. For the first time, I truly began to understand how I could actually love God with all of me—heart, soul, mind, and strength.

With the help of the Holy Spirit, good friends, a great counselor, and *a lot* of books, I slowly began finding the answers I needed to assemble my life back together—but not as it was before. I didn't want the life I had before. To the best of my ability, I wanted to have a moment-by-moment relationship with the Holy Spirit that

---

* I have cited the many quotes and ideas I learned from these authors where I use their words verbatim, but in truth I was so moved and changed by their works that their influence is present on every page.

shaped my deepest desires, beliefs, emotions, and thoughts, and as a pastor, I wanted to help other people experience that too.

Change is Possible

While you may not face crippling episodes of fear, you do have feelings, thoughts, or actions you wish you could change—we all do. Ever since Adam and Eve sinned, human beings are born with a feeling of inadequacy that won't go away. You try everything imaginable to fix yourself, but each attempt eventually makes you feel more helpless and ashamed. The good news is God loves you as you are. The broken, dysfunctional, inadequate version of you is completely and utterly loved by God. But the better news is, you don't have to stay the way you are.

Imagine for a moment a life that feels unhurried and unworried—a life that exudes patience, peace, and freedom from the obsession over people's opinions of you. A life of genuine humility that serves others without keeping score. A life of true contentment, not striving to prove something. A life free from secret sins and resentment. The life I'm describing was modeled for us by Jesus Christ, and it is available to everyone who decides to follow Him.

Loving God with all your heart, soul, mind, and strength, and truly loving your neighbor, requires more than church attendance—it requires character change. You have to become a different *kind* of person, with the awareness and vocabulary to know what the Holy Spirit is doing throughout the moments of your day.

You won't find quick fixes or gimmicks in the pages that follow. Instead, you will learn ancient Christian wisdom that, when practiced, will help you become the new person the Bible says you can be. You will feel resistance along the way, because layer upon layer of life experience is embedded in your body, influenced by a world set against God, and so even after you come to faith, your tendencies don't immediately follow your spiritual desires. A life led by His spirit will look different than the lives of those around you. It's a life guided by a different set of values, a life that pushes against the cultural norms of speed, consumption, and progress.

You will not find a deeply satisfying relationship with God the same way you find a destination on your smartphone. No, it will feel more like the way you find a good fishing spot—trial and error, experience, advice, and practice. Your old way of life only begins to yield as you participate in a relationship with the Holy Spirit, choice by choice. It's not magical or natural, and it requires intentional effort and practice, but Jesus already did the hardest part by defeating the power of sin on the cross.

The goal of this book is to help you move beyond an unfulfilling or underwhelming religion that has very little effect on your daily life. It's broken into two parts—*Foundations* and *Practices*—to help you experience a deeply rewarding relationship with Jesus that transforms your soul.

Part 1, *Foundations*, will help you understand why it's so hard to change. You will learn how to recognize the dysfunctional cycles and habits that keep you frustrated and inconsistent. Most importantly, you will be compelled to embrace emotional health *and* spiritual depth together, in your journey to experience deep change.

Part 2 teaches you four practices: *Feel Your Feelings, Face Your*

Past, *Change Your Habits*, and *Embrace Your Limits*. As you slow down and develop an awareness for God's presence in your life, you will begin to experience a more personal, moment-by-moment, relationship with Him.

The purpose of everything you will learn is not self-improvement, though your life will improve. Like Lewis said, "improvement is not redemption." The purpose is to be like Jesus in both deed and essence. But in order to experience that kind of life, you have to move beyond checking the boxes of religious participation and invite the Holy Spirit into the deepest parts of your life. The invitation Jesus gave 2,000 years ago is still available to us today.

> "Come to me, all of you who are weary and carry heavy burdens, and I will give you rest. Take my yoke upon you. Let me teach you, because I am humble and gentle at heart, and you will find rest for your souls. For my yoke is easy to bear, and the burden I give you is light."

Who better to teach us than the only person to ever fully love God with all His heart, soul, mind, and strength, and love His neighbor as himself? Of course, He was sinless, and we are not, but we can experience a life of transformation and a deep relationship with God as we make the effort to become more like Him.

As we begin this journey together, let's start with a prayer and invite the Holy Spirit to work deep within us.

A SOUL WITH WINGS

Oh Lord, when I compare my life to the life You lived,
I barely recognize any similarities.

You were active,
  but never hurried.
You were generous,
  but expected nothing in return.
You were present,
  but never distracted or annoyed.
You were tempted,
  but never gave in.
You were rejected,
  but never defensive.
You walked this earth with an ease and contentment I do not possess,
  but I want to.

I want to experience the life, power, and presence of Jesus
  in the day-to-day moments of my life.
Get past my defenses,
  my excuses,
  my concerns.
Gently open my soul and speak Your truth that will set me free.
Teach me Your way of life.

Amen.

PART 1
Foundations

CHAPTER ONE

Defining Normal

"I always believed any sin was easily rectified if only you let Jesus Christ into your heart, but here it gets complicated."
- **Leah Price** *The Poisonwood Bible*

If you want to become more like Jesus, you have to start by understanding yourself. This is easier said than done, but it is where the journey for deep change must begin.

It may seem like an odd starting point. Shouldn't you begin with learning more about Jesus? Joining a Bible study? Finding a good Bible reading plan? In my experience, most Christians have more than enough information about the life of Christ. They can tell you about His birth and death, His parables, and the miracles of turning water to wine, feeding 5,000, walking on water, and more. We're not uninformed—we know what Jesus did, but we struggle to do the same.

While Bible study is important, the greatest challenge to becoming like Jesus is not a lack of knowledge, but a lack of *self-knowledge*. We can't simply attempt to do what He did; we also have to examine *why* He was able to do it. What internal qualities did He possess that we lack?

When God revealed Himself to us, He did it in a human body. Ironically, it's far easier to believe in an invisible God than in a visible one. We rarely think about Jesus as a real human being with thoughts, feelings, and motivations. "Our tendency is to either reduce Him to morals or platitudes, or sentimentalize Him into entertainment. Most of us alternate between the two, and our lives remain unchanged." We emphasize His actions, but we rarely think about His character—the *kind* of person He was. For example, Jesus refused to defend Himself in the face of His accusers, but it wasn't because He learned how to hold His tongue; it was because He felt no need to react or be defensive. During a terrifying storm in the middle of the night, Jesus was able to sleep soundly, not because He was oblivious, but because He possessed a non-anxious presence, regardless of His circumstances.

This is a fundamental and common error in attempting to live the Christian life—you attempt to change what you do, but rarely change what you *want* to do. So you try to hold your tongue when you really want to defend yourself, or you try to act calm when you really want to scream. You try to be more patient, loving, kind, and self-controlled, instead of becoming the *kind* of person who is patient, loving, kind, and self-controlled. There is something to be said for mustering the willpower to overcome your instincts, but as you know by now, you can only act like someone you're not for so long. Eventually your character is revealed by your actions and reactions.

The Christian life is one of character change—being remade

from the inside out. We want the Holy Spirit to remake us into the kind of person who looks, sees, feels, and responds more and more like Jesus would if He was in our exact circumstance. As long as you try to change your behavior without understanding why you behave the way you do, your desire to change will be hijacked by your internal beliefs, which have run beneath the surface of your life for so long that you are oblivious to their dominant power.

Peter Scazzero, author of *Emotionally Healthy Spirituality*, has been one of the leading modern voices on this topic. He says, "...it wasn't until I understood that these beneath-the-surface components of my life had not been transformed by Jesus that I discovered the inseparable link between emotional health and spiritual maturity—that it is not possible to be spiritually mature while remaining emotionally immature."

This is where deep change occurs—at the intersection of spiritual depth and emotional health. (See image 1.1) Traditionally, churches emphasize spiritual depth alone, but this runs the risk of leaving you informed and unchanged. Has your relationship with Jesus addressed your deep internal wounds and sin patterns? Have you become a different person in private? Unfortunately, many Christians remain stunted at an immature level of spiritual and emotional development because they overestimate the power of their intentions and underestimate the power of their past.

Your relationship with Jesus does not begin with a blank canvas. Yes, your sins are forgiven, and in God's eyes, you are as perfect as Jesus. But you also have a lifetime of tendencies, desires, hurts, and habits that have created your identity and are keeping you stuck at

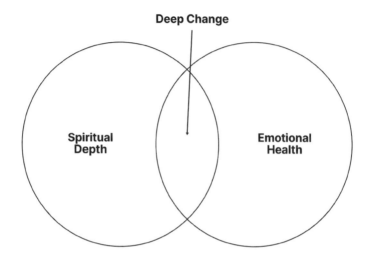

Image 1.1

the status quo. The good news, though, is that the Gospel means we can live a life that's different from what is given to us biologically, environmentally, and economically.

The word identity comes from the Latin words *essentitas*, which means "being," and *identidem*, which means "repeatedly." Your identity is literally your "repeated beingness." So each time you repeat a behavior or a thought, you are reinforcing who you believe you are. To be clear, it's not who God says you are, but it's who you believe you are. Consider all the repeated behaviors in your lifetime—the way you attract attention, spend money, handle conflict, and show love, just to name a few. Every time you act like you, you are confirming that you are who you think you are—you have proof of it. No wonder it's so hard to change.

This helps explain Christians who faithfully attend church, read their Bible, and strive to live moral lives, but still avoid conflict, feel like a failure, neglect their family, are overly critical, live with constant fear or anxiety, are unable to manage money, or struggle with the same sins of their youth. It's possible to experience salvation but not transformation because you never allow the Holy Spirit access to the deepest parts of your interior life. Is it because you don't want to change? Of course not! It's because your emotional dysfunction is familiar to you.

According to science, in a way, you can feel your thoughts. Some thoughts feel easy, like imagining words that rhyme with "hat" or listening to repetitive pop music. But sometimes thinking feels like work, like imagining words that rhyme with "strategy," listening to jazz music without a time signature, or processing complex emotions.

The human tendency is to avoid thinking about things that challenge your brain, so you continuously search for the easiest experiences and explanations—the ones that are most familiar. You are always trying to give your brain a break by neatly categorizing events and confirming what you thought all along.

Wanting to think easy thoughts is called *fluency*. It's why the music you listened to as a kid always causes nostalgia, and why your favorite foods and sports teams stay your favorite. It also contributes to racist views and gender bias—what's most familiar is most convenient. This means that in order to change deeply, you must confront what feels most natural.

Familiar Patterns and Predictable Reactions

So how can you identify the familiar tendencies, feelings, habits, and influences that are sabotaging your spiritual growth? One of the best ways is through spiritual self-reflection, or meditation. The goal is simply to be quiet and still enough to follow the example of David in Psalm 139, when he prayed, "Search me, God, and know my heart…" As you learn the practices of *feeling your feelings* and *embracing your limits*, you will create the time, vocabulary, and awareness to be sensitive to what the Holy Spirit is trying to teach you. For now, though, let's begin by reflecting on the repeating patterns and familiar reactions that seem to occur in your life by default.

One reason it's so hard to recognize your unhealthy tendencies is because they don't feel unhealthy at all—they feel normal. When unhealthy behavior, like anger, abandonment, or addiction, is modeled by your family, or your immature actions, like sarcasm, passive aggressive behavior, or blaming are affirmed, these behaviors become instinctual, and it's hard to see just how detrimental they are. This causes you to view your bad habits through the best possible lens, deflect blame, and rationalize your misery as random misfortune.

If you look closely enough, you will discover that you don't have a lot of problems, you have a few problems that repeat over and over. See if any of these examples sound familiar:

» Sarah and Michael have been incredibly stressed lately. Michael's hours increased at work, and the overtime pay is nice, but he's home less, which makes it challenging for Sarah to manage her job and the kids' schedules, plus trying to take care of her sick father. Most nights they end up fighting about feeling tired and alone. Sarah wishes Michael was home more, and Michael wishes Sarah was more appreciative of how hard he works to provide for the family. But both of them agree things will eventually slow down and they'll be able to enjoy the pace of life again. "It's just a season," they keep telling themselves. But if Sarah and Michael could identify the familiar patterns and predictable reactions in their life, they would realize that every stressful and crazy season has led into another crazy season. The truth is, neither of them can remember the last time they didn't feel overwhelmed—stress and busyness are *normal*.

» Brianna's last boyfriend was a jerk, and all her friends are so thankful the relationship is over. She decided she is done with relationships for a while. "God will bring me the right person; I'm not going to jump in so quickly again," she keeps telling herself. But if Brianna was honest enough to examine the familiar patterns and predictable reactions in her life, she would have to admit that she rarely stays single for very long, and every past relationship got too serious too quickly. She commits too soon and it always ends badly—unhealthy relationships are *normal*.

» Lindsey is highly respected by her peers as an accomplished professional, but whenever she goes home to visit her parents, she feels small, insecure, and defensive. At her office she's in charge, but around her parents she still feels like a little girl afraid to disappoint them, so she apologizes constantly, has trouble voicing her opinion, and strives to keep the peace. She hopes one day to be successful and confident enough to stand her ground, but if Lindsey was honest enough to spot the familiar patterns and predictable reactions in her life, she would have to admit that no matter what she accomplishes, it never gets better—feeling insignificant is *normal*.

The examples are endless, and we all have them. You're certain you'll feel content once you buy your new home. After this sports season, you're going to commit to fewer activities. You're not going to work so many hours after you get the promotion, or you won't be worried once your savings account reaches a certain balance. The painful truth is most of your life is a rerun—discontentment, busyness, overworking, and fear are normal.

Take a moment and review your life. Are you less busy than you were five years ago? Are you less angry? Less fearful? Less stressed? Are you relying less on caffeine, alcohol, or drugs? Probably not. Life speeds up, bad habits grow, and flaws magnify. Our sinful patterns and unhealthy reactions are really just symptoms of the struggles that occur beneath the surface of our life, and the roots run deep. We ward off feelings of insecurity, anxiety, fear, and loneliness with distractions like kids' sports, pursuing career success, binging TV shows, drinking, drugs, eating, unhealthy relationships, and scrolling on our phone.

DEFINING NORMAL

There are many reasons our spiritual growth stalls and we get caught in these cycles of dysfunction. Some are more complicated than others, and we will talk about those reasons more in the next chapter, but no matter how hopeless you may feel, you can be certain that dysfunction doesn't have to be normal. God wants a new normal for you—a life of spiritual depth and emotional health; of "green pastures" and "still waters" as described in Psalm 23.

With the help of the Holy Spirit and the practices you will learn in this book, you can experience a relationship with Jesus that changes you at the deepest levels of your life, but you have to start by admitting your current condition isn't an exception—it's normal. Any attempt at deep change will require incredible courage and honesty, but if you're willing to invite the Holy Spirit into your interior life, He will help you, and you can find the freedom, depth, and health you desperately long for.

Peter Scazzero calls defining normal "acknowledging your shadow." He argues that you can't change what you are unaware of, "…but once you acknowledge your shadow—both its root causes and its expressions—its power over you is diminished if not broken."

So let's end this chapter by asking the Holy Spirit to help you recognize the familiar patterns and predictable reactions in your life. Is there a consistent feeling you feel or a statement you repeat to yourself? These are clues to the emotional barriers keeping you from the spiritual growth you desire. I've provided a one-sentence template to help you begin defining normal.

When _____ I usually _____ and I end up _____.

Some examples:
- When *I get extra money* I usually *spend it quickly on stuff I don't need*, and I end up *feeling angry with myself for not having it when I need it.*
- When *people try to get close to me*, I usually *pull away* and I end up *feeling alone*.
- When *I start dating someone* I usually *give them all my energy and attention* and I end up *isolating myself from my friends and family*.
- When *I get bored*, I usually *do things I swore to myself I wouldn't do anymore*, and I end up *feeling defeated and ashamed that I can't seem to stop*.
- When *I walk into a room*, I usually *assume people won't like me* and I end up *hiding*.

Before moving on to the next chapter, take a few deep breaths and ask the Holy Spirit to help you identify the familiar patterns and predictable reactions in your life using the sentence above. Pray the words of Psalm 139 before you start:

Search me, God, and know my heart;
test me and know my anxious thoughts.
See if there is any offensive way in me,
and lead me in the way everlasting.

Chapter Summary

- » The greatest challenge to becoming like Jesus is not a lack of knowledge, but a lack of self-knowledge.

- » The Christian life is one of character change—being remade from the inside out. We want the Holy Spirit to remake us into the kind of person who looks, sees, feels, and responds more and more like Jesus would if He was in our exact circumstance.

- » Your relationship with Jesus does not begin with a blank canvas. Yes, your sins are forgiven, and in God's eyes, you are as perfect as Jesus. But you also have a lifetime of tendencies, desires, hurts, and habits that have created your identity and are keeping you stuck at the status quo.

- » When unhealthy behavior, like anger, abandonment, or addiction, is modeled by your family, or your immature actions, like sarcasm, passive aggressive behavior, or blaming are affirmed, these behaviors become instinctual, and it's hard to see just how detrimental they are.

- » Is there a consistent feeling you feel or a statement you repeat to yourself? These are clues to the emotional barriers keeping you from the spiritual growth you desire.

CHAPTER TWO

Why You Want What You Want

"You will know the truth and the truth will set you free"

- Jesus

If you're still reading this book, that means you had the courage to face your shadow and begin defining normal. That's not easy, so I want to commend you for your courage. Hopefully you were able to identify some of the familiar patterns and predictable reactions in your life. If so, you are on your way to experiencing deep change. The next question is *why*? Why do you instinctively do the things you do again and again, especially when those actions make you feel worse about yourself or are not helping you become the person you want to be? Consider the following examples:

» Lauren is one of the kindest people you will ever meet. She is helpful, encouraging, and always there for her friends. She plans all the bridal and baby showers and always brings the best food to the parties. She seems to always be available, and always goes the extra mile to make sure her friends have what they need. On the surface, Lauren is a loving, considerate, helpful friend, but beneath the surface, Lauren harbors feelings of resentment and anger. Her whole life, she has made sure everyone is taken care of, but she doesn't feel like anyone cares about her as much as she cares about them. Lauren wants to be loved, and believes the way she can attain that love is through serving others, so she keeps serving and helping, hoping to finally get what she wants, all the while growing more hurt, bitter, and angry.

» Maria is the definition of a high achiever. As a wife and mom, she never lets anything fall through the cracks. Her house stays clean and the kids' clothes are always washed and folded. She makes their lunch in the morning, has dinner ready when her husband gets home, and in her free time volunteers at their school and her church. It appears to everyone that Maria is dependable, responsible, efficient, and confident, but beneath the surface, she battles intense feelings of inadequacy. No matter how much she accomplishes, she always feels as if she could have done more. She desperately wants to prove her worth, so she keeps striving, committing, and adding to her to-do list, hoping that one day she will feel like she does enough and is enough.

» Chad is a pastor who is loved by his congregation. He is young, charismatic, a great preacher, and has helped the church grow dramatically in the three short years he's been there. He is confident and articulate, and he is respected and applauded among his peers for his results, but Chad is keeping an unsustainable pace. He never takes a day off. He's the first one to show up and the last one to leave, and he is pushing his volunteers to match his intensity, causing many of them to feel burned out and used. He tells the church it's about reaching people for Jesus, and it is, but it's also about his own desperate need for attention and affirmation. As long as the church is growing, he feels validated and important.

These stories help us see how many of the things we wish we could change about ourselves are the very actions we instinctively perform, and have been performing for a long time—Lauren always helps, Maria always accomplishes, and Chad is always pushing. So why do we do it, and why does it seem so difficult to stop? This chapter will help you understand the reasons behind your dysfunctional patterns, discover your underlying motivation, and recognize how your actions are merely an attempt to gain what you want most in life.

For now, let's start with this fundamental question: what do you want? What is the scenario or outcome that you've rehearsed in your mind, and swear that if you had it, you would feel truly happy, complete, whole, unafraid, or secure? Think about it.

In my experience, this is a difficult question to answer, especially if it's the first time you've attempted it. It's difficult for two reasons. The first is because our desires are buried so deep within our interior lives that they are often disguised—in fact, if you try to identify someone's desires based solely on their actions, you will almost always guess incorrectly. For example, a person who desires love and connection may be incredibly withdrawn, and a person who desperately wants affirmation may act excessively arrogant.

The second reason it's difficult to answer is because many people have simply never thought about it. Sure, you've thought, "I want a million dollars," or "I want to have sex," or "I want to start my own

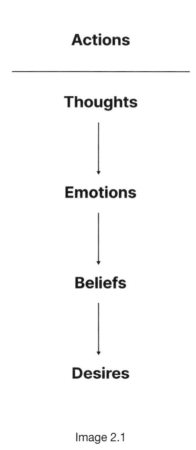

Image 2.1

business," and these answers are accurate, but they are insufficient. In truth, what you really want is what you believe a million dollars, or sex, or entrepreneurship will get you. Your instinctual answer is a good starting point, but your greater desires are still hiding somewhere deeper in your soul.

In order to identify what you want most, you have to recognize the structure of your soul—how you think, how you feel, and what you believe. If this sounds exhausting or intimidating, it's only because it's foreign to you. As you learn to *feel your feelings*, *face your past*, *change your habits*, and *embrace your limits*, this type of self-awareness will become much more natural.

The Structure of Your Soul

In its simplest form, your soul is the part of you that connects all the other parts of you. It's the sum of your deepest desires, beliefs, emotions, and thoughts.[*] (See image 2.1) What makes your soul hard to define is that it mostly operates without conscious supervision. Like a computer operating system, you tend to only notice it when it malfunctions. When you don't get what you want, or life doesn't work the way you think it should, your emotions and thoughts can become erratic, and you experience differing degrees of despair. This almost always leads to action meant to ease your discomfort.

---

[*] I first learned about the Structure of the Soul model from marriage and family therapist Brandon Smith. I have adapted some of his original model, but the general concept is the same that our actions (or physical self) are a direct reflection of our interior life.

The Structure of the Soul

Actions: Your actions are the public evidence of your choices. They're the physical side of you that people can see and interpret. While you are technically free to do whatever you want, in practice, your choices are the result of relentless pressure from your interior life. This explains why your best intentions always seem to be sabotaged. Yes, you have free will, but by the time you make a choice, you have been influenced by your desires, beliefs, emotions, and thoughts. This is why Jesus said, "For whatever is in your heart determines what you say." Everything made public was first influenced by your private life.

Thoughts: Your thoughts are the ideas and opinions you have throughout the day, and these really add up. Some studies suggest you think as many as 6,200 thoughts per day! This includes everything—from benign observations about the world around you, like "I like that shade of blue" or "Cute dog," to daily decisions, like "I need to do laundry" or "I want a cheeseburger," and even opinions of yourself and the people you encounter, like "I'm ugly," "No one notices me," or "They are stupid." Your thoughts are shaped by your emotions, and they are the last step before you act. Contrary to popular opinion, you are not helpless or powerless against your thoughts—you have the ability to influence the things your brain focuses on. The Bible calls this "setting your mind."

Emotions: Your emotions are instinctive internal reactions based on your circumstances and surroundings. We are all emotional beings, including people who claim not to be. At any given moment throughout your day, you feel a certain way about something. We'll talk more in depth about this in the *Feel Your Feelings* practice. But for now, just know that whether or not you realize it or understand what to call them, you feel emotions, and those emotions shape your thoughts.

Beliefs: Your deeply-held beliefs are the stories you tell yourself, and the unwritten rules you live your life by. You tell yourself stories about money, relationships, happiness, status, and many other things. You have a way you believe the world works, and this creates your expectations. Beliefs are different from thoughts in that they include an assumption of truth. It's the difference between "I want to be rich" (thought) and "rich people are happy" (belief). Your beliefs are your assumptions for how life will go, and they can lead to discomfort when life doesn't go according to plan.

Desires: Your desires are the outcomes you want, and they motivate you to perform your responsibilities. Depending on your religious background, you might assume desires are bad, but they're not. Our deepest longings and impulses are given to us by God to draw us to Him. Of course, they can become perverted and deflected, but as long as you think of desires as inherently bad, your shame will keep you from discovering what's true about you.

So let's recap: What you want most (desire), determines what you believe is true about life (belief), and that determines how you feel (emotions) and think (thoughts) about your life, and ultimately determines what you do (actions).

> It's worth pointing out that your interior life isn't as clean cut and simple as these explanations. You are a complex human being, which means there are more things happening in your brain at a moment of decision than you can count. You can't live your life analyzing every moment—it's both exhausting and narcissistic—but if you're willing to think about it long enough and be honest with yourself, you will find that your choices are deeply intertwined with what you want and how you believe you can get it. Simply put, you do things you don't want to do because you feel ways you don't want to feel, and those feelings come from trying to keep or get what you want most. Each time you try to make the right choice, the relentless pressure of your interior life makes it feel impossible.

In his book, *The Gift of Being Yourself*, author and psychologist David Benner tells the story of a pastor named Stuart who came to see him for a sexual addiction. Stuart felt incredibly guilty for his long-standing use of pornography, but also felt totally helpless to change it.

Benner and Stuart started down a dark and difficult path of self-understanding, and they discovered that behind the sexual addiction was not just a reservoir of lust, but a longing for intimacy. In fantasy, he sought a different type of intimacy that a real relationship did not demand of him. More importantly, Stuart discovered a high degree of resentment and a strong sense of entitlement—a feeling that he deserved something better than he was experiencing in his marriage.

By facing his past, he was able to realize he had felt overlooked in a larger family of six siblings. He was deeply bitter that no one recognized how special he was. He had been the responsible one who took care of everyone else, but no one seemed to appreciate his efforts. Stuart learned to cover his resentment with a mask of false humility, but beneath that mask, he was consumed by bitterness. Pride made him believe he deserved special treatment, and when he didn't receive it, he withdrew in hurt and anger. This led to a sense of being cut off and deprived of intimacy, which in turn led to his attraction to pornography.

Image 2.2

Confronting the depths of his pride and sense of entitlement was enormously difficult, but "discovering and accepting that he longed for intimacy, not simply sexual gratification, was transformational."

Stuart's story shows how your "soul operating system" directs your life inconspicuously, and it helps explain how the actions we want to change have to be addressed at each level of our soul.

While you may not struggle with addiction, the previous chapter helped you identify your own dysfunctional patterns. Like Stuart, you must identify the deepest desires that motivate your repeated actions and reactions—why you want what you want. (See image 2.2)

Good Things Gone Wrong

The Greek word commonly used in the Bible for "desire" is *epithumia*, which in English is translated as "over desires." Think of it this way—it's not that you necessarily want bad things, it's more that you want things too badly. This can give you a new view of sin and the role it plays in your life. Traditionally, sin is thought of in terms of immoral actions, but now you can see that those actions are just attempts to gain control of your interior life. This is why Jesus could compare anger and murder as equals. Of course the physical consequences are not the same, but the effect on the soul is—anger and murder give each person the same sense of justice. They both make us feel like we're taking matters into our own hands, rather than letting things happen to us. As long as you believe that your behavior, rather than your desires, is the best gauge to define your love for God, you'll never understand why Jesus treats an internal feeling and an external action with the same weight. However, once you begin to accept that the soul is the center of your spiritual life, you will begin to grasp how deep change results in joyful submission, rather than the usual miserable compliance.

What if you thought about sin less as actions and more as unhealthy ways you try to find self-esteem? Promiscuous sex is an attempt to gain love, affirmation, power, or safety. Lying is a way to keep power, control, or your reputation. Gossiping is a way to feel superior or powerful, or impress someone. As we begin to identify our deepest desires, we also begin to see how our actions are attempts to give us what we believe makes us most lovable or valuable. In this way, you can trace every sin in your life back to your deepest desires—you're trying to attain them or cope without them. This is what James was describing when he said "our own desires entice us, drag us away, and give birth to sinful actions."

It would be much easier to recognize our "over desires" if they were only evident in our vices, but because we are sinful people, we can make even the purest things self-serving. Before you move forward, it is absolutely imperative that you begin to recognize how your desires influence your life. If not, you will simply manipulate every behavior, even the "good" ones, to get what you want. We are masters at disguising our unhealthy tendencies as virtues. That's why you can't just *feel your feelings*, *face your past*, *change your habits*, and *embrace your limits*. Without understanding your deepest desires and deeply-held beliefs, you will use noble activity and spiritual practice to disguise your pursuit. But once you know that you are motivated by a need for control, or safety, or importance, or anything else, you can spot how even your noble acts and spiritual pursuits can be taken over by the sinful parts of you. The good news is that your soul can be renewed—with the help of the Holy Spirit, your desires and beliefs can change.

Let's end this chapter by trying to answer the question: What do you want? What is the scenario you imagine in your head that would make your fears, inconveniences, bitterness, and feelings of inadequacy go away?

Some examples might be:
- I want to win the lottery
- I want to be famous
- I want to be skinny
- I want to be married
- I want to have children
- I want a new car
- I want a new house
- I want my boss to lose his job
- I want my dad to apologize for leaving our family
- I want to leave my spouse
- I want to quit my job
- I want to look younger
- I want to live in a good neighborhood

Your answers to this question (you can have more than one) are a great starting point. Let me ask you one more question: *Why?*

Take a few moments and ask the Holy Spirit to help you answer honestly about why you want each thing you want. Don't be in a hurry. You are learning the truth about some of the deepest parts of your soul. It can feel scary, and shame will certainly try to make you feel terrible for being honest, but remember that Jesus said, "the truth will set you free." You may not feel free immediately, but you are well on your way to believing God loves the real you.

Chapter Summary

» Our deepest desires are masters of disguise. In order to identify what you want most, you have to recognize how you think, how you feel, and what you believe.

» Your soul is the part of you that connects all the other parts of you. It's the sum of your deepest desires, beliefs, emotions, and thoughts.

» What you want most (desire), determines what you believe is true about life (belief), and that determines how you feel (emotions) and think (thoughts) about your life, and ultimately determines what you do (actions).

» It is absolutely imperative that you begin to recognize how your desires influence your life. If not, you will simply manipulate every behavior, even the "good" ones, to get what you want.

» What do you want? What is the scenario you imagine in your head that would make your fears, inconveniences, bitterness, and feelings of inadequacy go away?

CHAPTER THREE

Nothing to Prove

> "God loves human beings...Not an ideal
> human, but human beings as they are..."
> -Dietrich Bonhoffer

As you begin to learn the four practices, the most natural thing in the world will be to add them to the list of all the other requirements you feel you must perform for God—something else you need to become really good at—but you don't have to do that.

There's a story in the Gospel of Matthew about a young man who approached Jesus one day and asked, "Teacher, what good deed must I do to have eternal life?" Jesus responded by encouraging the young man to keep the commandments given in the Old Testament—don't kill, steal, or commit adultery—to which the man replied, "I have obeyed all these. What else must I do?"

I've always found this exchange interesting. If the young man had kept all of the commandments required for eternal life, why didn't he feel like he possessed it? If he was obeying all the rules, why did he still feel he was missing something?

There's another story Jesus tells in Luke about a father and two sons. The younger son left and wasted his inheritance, and eventually was welcomed back home despite his reckless choices. But this infuriated the older brother. He asked his father, "After how hard I've worked for you all these years, why don't you celebrate me like my irresponsible brother?"

Similar to the first young man, the older brother had done all the right things and performed all of his duties, but still lacked confidence that his father was pleased with him.

These stories perfectly describe the struggle so many Christians feel in their pursuit of a meaningful relationship with God. We want to know, what *must* we do? We serve and we strive, but we still feel we're lacking something. It turns out moral excellence performed for approval does not increase your self-worth; on the contrary, it makes you feel more insecure, judgemental, and lifeless. You don't feel the fullness of eternal life or a closeness with your heavenly father—you're not convinced He approves of you. There is a nagging feeling of inadequacy. You wonder, "Am I good enough for God?" There's this sense that it's not enough to be saved, you have to *really* mean it.

Of course, Christians should have a genuine faith, but because genuine faith is so hard to quantify, we typically measure only by the standards we deem important. If you're a *real* Christian you will be really strong, or really patriotic, or really generous, or really available, or really energetic or prayerful or committed, or whatever else the person with the microphone is passionate about. We volunteer, give, attend, have our quiet time, complete our Bible reading plan, and join a small group, and we wonder, "What else *must* I do?" It's exhausting.

I love the way Eugene Peterson translated Jesus' instructions to pray:

> "Here's what I want you to do: Find a quiet, secluded place so you won't be tempted to role-play before God. Just be there as simply and honestly as you can manage. The focus will shift from you to God, and you will begin to sense his grace."

We are all tempted to role-play before God. The thought of a more honest, introspective, or patient spirituality feels strange at best, and sacrilegious at worst. For many modern Christians in a technological age, quiet feels like lethargy and reverence feels like boredom, so inevitably we feel pressure to do more than Jesus asks us to—pressure to be more, feel more, say more. But God doesn't want that for you. He wants you to sense His grace.

The thing about grace is that it can't be earned; it can only be received. As long as you continue to strive to feel good enough for God—to prove that you are a good Christian He can be proud of—you will never sense His grace, only more pressure, and the last thing you need is more pressure.

Jesus gives you an invitation: "Come to me, all of you who are weary and carry heavy burdens, and I will give you rest." It's pretty simple—He does all the giving, and all you have to do is show up. This is harder than it should be. We become so busy trying to do *for* God that we never sense His grace. We struggle to believe we can show up empty-handed, but that is the beauty of the Gospel—the only thing you have to give Him is your sin.

This isn't to say that your attempts for spiritual depth and emotional health will come naturally to you. They won't. If along the way you think, "I'm not very good at this," it's okay. Jesus is teaching you a new way of life, and it must be learned, but—and this is crucial—it cannot be *earned*. The deep change you desire will require effort and practice, but you have nothing to prove, only everything to receive.

Ironically, the more you try to earn God's love, the less you feel loved. Instead, you will feel more insecure, ashamed, discouraged, tired, or needy. You will struggle to hold up "your end of the deal." You will convince yourself that all your efforts are for God, but they're not; you're doing them for yourself—to convince yourself that He approves of you.

It's Not For God

Charles Spurgeon used to tell a story about a king who ruled over everything in a land. One day a gardener grew an enormous carrot. He took it to the king and said, "My lord, this is the greatest carrot I've ever grown or ever will grow; therefore, I want to present it to you as a token of my love and respect for you."

The king was touched and discerned the man's heart, so as the man turned to go, the king said, "Wait! You are clearly a good steward of the earth. I want to give a plot of land to you freely as a gift, so you can garden it all." The gardener was amazed and delighted and went home rejoicing.

But there was a nobleman at the king's court who overheard all this, and he said, "My! If that is what you get for a carrot, what if you gave the king something better?" The next day, the nobleman came before the king, leading a handsome black stallion. He bowed low and said, "My lord, I breed horses, and this is the greatest horse I've ever bred or ever will; therefore, I want to present it to you as a token of my love and respect for you." But the king discerned his heart, so he said, "Thank you," took the horse, and simply dismissed him.

The nobleman was perplexed, and the king explained, "That gardener was giving me the carrot, but you were giving yourself the horse."

Once you begin to sense His grace, you stop feeling like you *have* to, and you begin to want to. The truth is you don't have to do anything for God, but once you believe that, you will do anything for God.

Do you believe that? Isn't there some part of you that wants to reject it? Wouldn't being free of any obligations demotivate someone from trying? Maybe. But if unconditional love kills your motivation for effort, then fear is the only reason you were trying, and fear will never transform your life.

The opportunity before you is to learn how to posture yourself before God, slow down, and sense His grace. The Holy Spirit is involved, so there are no steps or formulas, and while some methods are more beneficial than others, technically there is no right or wrong way. You are invited to learn the ways of Christian men and women who have gone before you. Some days will be better than others. Occasionally you will experience the transcendent presence of God, and other days you will be interrupted by spilling your coffee or the kids waking up, but it doesn't matter. Simply show up as honestly as you can manage, ready to receive.

I hope by now you have identified familiar patterns and predictable reactions in your life, and you have begun to understand what motivates you. If not, you may want to go back and reread the last two chapters before reading further.

If you're ready to take the next step toward spiritual depth and emotional health, let's move forward and learn how to *feel your feelings*, *face your past*, *change your habits*, and *embrace your limits*.

Chapter Summary

» Moral excellence performed for approval does not increase your self-worth, but rather makes you feel more insecure, judgemental, and lifeless. You will convince yourself that all your efforts are for God, but they're not; you're doing them for yourself—to convince yourself that He approves of you.

» Jesus is teaching you a new way of life. It cannot be earned, but it must be learned. The deep change you desire will require effort and practice, but you have nothing to prove, only everything to receive.

» Once you begin to sense God's grace, you stop feeling like you have to, and you begin to want to. The truth is you don't have to do anything for God, but once you believe that, you will do anything for God.

PART 2

Practices

PRACTICE #1

Feel Your Feelings

CHAPTER FOUR

Permission to Be Human

"The hardest thing of all to see is what is really there."
-J.A. Baker *The Peregrine*

"**I don't normally say things like this,** but I feel like I may be fighting against something demonic." That's what I told my counselor while working through the episodes of fear and anxiety I told you about earlier. "You could be, but probably not," my counselor replied. "It sounds like you're just becoming aware of emotions you have ignored for the last 37 years." And to think I was paying for this advice.

The truth is, it would have been a lot easier if my counselor would have just agreed with me and blamed my out-of-control spiral on the devil. That way, I could have called my grandmother for prayer and just held on until it passed. But he was right. This wasn't a demon, it was something even worse …*feelings*!

Most of my life I could explain how I felt in one of three ways:

perfectly fine, a little frustrated, or mildly amused. And that was pretty much it! My emotional knowledge and vocabulary was the equivalent of those three-packs of crayons they give kids with their menu at a restaurant. What I called "emotional stability" was really emotional ineptitude. Unintentionally, I had lived my life under the illusion that I just wasn't a very emotional person.

Of course, I am an emotional person, and so are you. I simply didn't have the awareness or vocabulary to understand what was happening beneath the surface of my life. Sadly, my spirituality had done very little to help me understand myself. My knowledge about God was growing, but my self-knowledge was lacking. What felt like a demon was really me admitting for the first time in my life that I was afraid—like, *really* afraid.

The first practice of deep change is *Feel Your Feelings*, and it's first for a reason. We tend to be good at putting the best possible spin on things, or at least ignoring the painful or most embarrassing parts of ourselves—you are never quite as healthy or confident as you appear. Until you recognize what you're experiencing in your interior life, any attempts to *face your past*, *change your habits*, or *embrace your limits* will be hijacked by denial or naive optimism.

It's important to remember that even if some people are less demonstrative than others, everyone is emotional. More importantly, everyone can improve their emotional intelligence. But our goal is not just emotional intelligence. We want to be more like Jesus in deed and essence, and in the words of Archbishop John Chrysostom, when you "find the door to your heart, you will discover it is the door to the kingdom of God."

Because we read the stories of Jesus with the knowledge that He is God, we tend to pass over His human experiences, but He did not walk the earth unresponsive. He had an interior life that reacted to His circumstances and surroundings. When He saw what had become of the business of the temple, He felt angry. When He interacted with the religious leaders, He was disappointed. When His friend died, He wept with sadness. When He thought about His crucifixion in the garden, He felt anxious. He experienced confrontation and He had expectations. Of all the ways God could have chosen to reveal Himself, He chose to be a human being. Don't rush past that. *Jesus is God as a human being.* That means being more like Jesus requires becoming more human, not less—more aware and comfortable with the "pain of being human." The questions we should be asking are: How was Jesus angry, but never passive aggressive? How was He disappointed, but never bitter? How did His anxiety not lead to hopelessness?

It's far too common to check the boxes of spiritual activity, but still never allow the Holy Spirit access to the deepest parts of who you are—to never experience the fullness of human life. Sadly, we embrace the faulty idea that Christianity requires you to be more spiritual and less human, and this keeps us from a more authentic, personal relationship with the Holy Spirit moment by moment. It's only when you learn the truth about God *and* yourself that change begins to happen, and the new person that God made you begins to emerge.

This is not a modern concept. It's actually as old as Christianity itself. St. Augustine asked, "How can you draw close to God when you are far from your own self?" and St. Teresa of Avila said, "Almost all problems in the spiritual life stem from a lack of self-knowledge."

Feeling your feelings is just the conscious practice of being aware of how moments throughout your day affect you internally—your heart, soul, mind, and strength. It requires a vocabulary and awareness to help you begin to fight against your deeply entrenched false self—the version of you that you believe God, and everyone else, needs you to be.

Fighting Your False Self

When I say "false self," I don't mean that you are intentionally living a double life. On the contrary, the life that you are currently living comes very naturally. A false self is a persona created early in life to help you feel safe, or important, or noticed. In your childhood, you discovered that you could secure love by presenting yourself in the most flattering light, so that's what you did, and continue to do. You portray the most lovable version of yourself to the world—the version you believe God and everyone else needs you to be. You work hard to sustain that identity, but it's exhausting to always be responsible, or funny, or sexy, or strong, or confident, or whoever else you have to be. Any emotions that conflict with what you believe makes you valuable are treated with hostility or flat out denial. Whatever identity you bring to the world that makes you feel worthwhile is the persona you bring to God, too, and vulnerability is too great a risk.

Most of the time, this false self has been functioning beneath the surface for so long that you don't recognize its dominance. But it overpowers the real you, with feelings and hurts that you may have never shown to God. Until you accept the truth about who you are, what you feel, and what you think, you will never expose your most vulnerable self to God. You will continue to take safe, inconsequential sins to Him for forgiveness, and ask Him for help with your endeavors, but you will never dare expose your weaknesses.

When was the last time you talked to God about your jealousy, or your need for attention, or your fear of failure? Many Christians have figured out how to "spend time with God" without having to address the hidden hurts and habits that keep them from deep change. "We are like farmers who keep adding fertilizer without admitting the existence of weeds and insects."

C.S. Lewis described it perfectly in his classic tale, *Screwtape Letters*, when Screwtape is advising his protege, Wormwood, on how to keep his human from experiencing spiritual progress.* "You must bring him to a condition in which he can practice self-examination for an hour without discovering any of those facts about himself which are perfectly clear to anyone who has ever lived in the same house with him or worked in the same office." Consider some of these examples:

» Rick is a present father who always shows up to his kids' events and activities, especially their games. As soon as they were able to walk, he started showing them how to shoot, throw, and

---

* Screwtape Letters is a satire written from the perspective of a demon, Screwtape, trying to train his nephew in the art of temptation and attempts to lead his "patient" away from God.

catch, and all the training paid off, because his kids are really good at sports. He never misses a game, and he makes sure they have all the resources they need to succeed. But if you saw Rick at one of their games, he wouldn't look like he was enjoying it, because he is always mad about something. He's mad at the coach for not playing his child enough, or he's mad at the referee for making a bad call, or he's mad at his kids for not giving enough effort. When the family gets in the car after the game, the first thing he brings up is how they could have limited their mistakes. Rick would tell you he is just trying to help them maximize their potential, and if he doesn't push them they will miss out on future opportunities, but Rick has never admitted to himself that his kids' wins and losses make him feel like a winner or a loser. Rick is a Christian who leads a small group for his church, but his faith has never forced him to face his feelings of inadequacy. He's never admitted to himself or God that a large part of his self-worth is attached to his children's achievements.

» Jimmy and his family have recently started attending a new church, and they love it. Unfortunately, this is the third new church they've attended in the last few years. If you ask Jimmy or his wife, they will tell you it's because God had led them to find another church where they were more spiritually challenged. But at each of their previous churches, there was conflict that caused them to make a change. At one church, their children weren't given speaking parts in the Christmas production, and at another, Jimmy had not been considered for a role as an elder. What Jimmy and his wife perceive as God leading them somewhere else is really just their fear of conflict. They consistently feel slighted, but have become proficient at spiritualizing away their emotional immaturity—leaving is easier than having a difficult conversation. Jimmy has been a Christian for a long time, but his faith has never forced him to admit to himself or God that he has a deep fear of rejection and longing for acceptance, which causes him to avoid conflict at all costs.

» Olivia is a good mom and a supportive wife, but if you asked her husband how he felt in their home, he would admit he felt like he was always getting reprimanded for something. He isn't perfect, but no matter how many good things he does, Olivia explodes in anger at the first sign of a mistake. If you asked her children, they would admit that they never feel like they can live up to her expectations. She only seems to notice the bad grades, or when their room isn't clean. Olivia would tell you she is just trying to keep her family organized and set her children up to succeed in life. She knows she can be a little grouchy sometimes, but it's because no one seems to care as much as she does. Olivia is a Christian who faithfully attends church. She wants to be a good mom and wife, but even more, she wants others to perceive her that way. Her faith has never forced her to admit to herself or God that she is deeply afraid of other people's opinions. She can't remember the last time she felt at peace because she lives with an impossible pressure to have the perfect family.

These stories help us see how we are highly skilled at self-deception. We're not intentionally lying to ourselves, but subconsciously we mask the truth by magnifying our strengths or deflecting responsibility. This is why it's crucial to feel your feelings.

Many Christians avoid their emotions because they believe it's the Christian thing to do. I can remember countless times when I heard Bible verses like, "The human heart is the most deceitful of all things, and desperately wicked." Whether stated explicitly or implied, the message was clear: "Don't listen to your heart!" Often, what the preacher meant was, "Don't make big decisions on a whim just because it feels right," and I agree, but that's not what it means to feel your feelings.

Modern Christianity has done a poor job of integrating the human body into our theology, but listening to your body and processing your emotions are actually crucial to the vitality of your spiritual life. We are drawn toward big ideas or "deep" truths, ignoring the physical realities of our faith, but God more commonly speaks to you through a knot in your stomach than a voice in the sky. Feeling your feelings is one of the best ways to experience God, and identify where you are embracing your false self.

Awareness and Confession

We can learn from the spiritual journey of Peter, one of Jesus' disciples—there was probably no other disciple who was more transformed during their time with Jesus. We will look at Peter more in the *Change Your Habits* practice, but there is something we can learn from him to help confront our self-deception. Like us, what made Peter strong also made him weak. He was bold and confident, often speaking up first or taking the lead in situations, but he was also hot-tempered and impulsive. The same instincts that caused him to step out of the boat and walk on the water toward Jesus also caused him to grab a sword and cut off the soldier's ear when Jesus was being arrested. If you asked Peter what he knew about himself after spending a few years with Jesus, he might have told you that he knew he could be too quick to act or that he spoke out of turn sometimes, but he would also have told you that he was growing in confidence and authority.

Even walking side by side with Jesus, Peter was unaware of how much he feared the opinions of others—and how susceptible he was to them. When Jesus predicted his denial, he swore, "I would never!" As is often the case, doubting Jesus was easier than doubting himself, but he was not as committed or invincible as he believed he was. In the heat of the moment, in the face of what felt like relentless pressure, he encountered his weakest and most despicable self. In denying Christ, Peter learned something about himself that he did not know before: he was more prideful and afraid than he ever imagined.

Like Peter, we tend to be blind to our vulnerabilities, and unknowingly deceive ourselves. Consider someone who is strong and confident but never able to embrace their weak or insecure self—they are forced to live a lie. "They must pretend that they *are* strong and confident, not simply that they *have* strong and confident parts or that under certain circumstances they *can be* strong and confident." Consequently, they will build their self-esteem by looking down on others who aren't as strong and confident as they are, and love people in a way that magnifies their strength and confidence but never exposes their vulnerabilities. The same is true for someone who refuses to face their deceitful self. They live an illusion regarding their own integrity, and are unaware of just how dishonest they are in the way they present themselves. Or someone who is unwilling to acknowledge their prideful self—they live in the illusion of false modesty, blind to how highly they view themselves compared to others.

With the help of *embracing your limits* and *changing your habits* to include silence and solitude, you can begin to create an awareness of what's happening in your interior life. You can invite the Holy Spirit into your self-reflection to help you identify how the events of the previous day, or even years, made you feel. Consider questions like: What am I angry about? What am I sad about? What feels uncertain right now? What condemnation am I feeling about my mistakes? What am I desiring that may be leading away from God's good plans for my life? This is a great way to create awareness of the condition of your soul.[**]

As David Benner points out, in general, 'what' questions (such as, What was I feeling? What disturbed me about that comment?

[**] I have provided a journal page you can use for your morning prayer time in Appendix A. Visit deepchangebook.com if you would like to print a digital copy.

What exactly made me anxious?) are better than 'why' questions (Why did I feel threatened? Why did that bother me?). Don't try to figure it out—simply *feel*. There is enormous power in admitting and naming your experiences. It's a holy moment. "Consciousness of sin, inadequacy, and unworthiness is a regular part of worship." You aren't what you should be, or even what you want to be, but you are completely loved by your heavenly father.

I must warn you, if this is the first time you've ever tried to identify and name your feelings, it can be challenging. In your frustration, you can convince yourself it's unnecessary and a waste of time, but you're simply learning how to be still and honest. No one is keeping score, and you don't have to be good at it. The point of self-reflection and meditation is not to simply be more introspective or intelligent, or to achieve some zen-like state. Spiritual transformation—being able to love God and your neighbor—is the goal. But you are only able to love people with all of their faults to the degree you believe you are loved by God with all of your faults too.

As you make it a practice to come to God as "simply and honestly as you can manage," you will begin to sense His grace. I love the way Richard Rohr explains it: "We cannot attain the presence of God because we're already totally in the presence of God. What's absent is awareness." This is the first practice in the deep change journey—awareness of the presence of God and the truth about the condition of your soul.

Deep change requires that you bring your true self to God. The *real* you—with feelings like anger, fear, jealousy, embarrassment, shame, and insecurity—feels so exposed, so vulnerable, so unworthy, that you wonder, "Why would God love a mess like me?" It's at that moment when, maybe for the first time, you finally grasp the Gospel. You are in fact a sinner, worse off than you ever imagined, but more loved than you could comprehend. You have nothing to offer. You need His grace, and now you're finally ready to receive it.

Rich Mullins, the famous Christian singer back in the '80s and '90s, used to say that when he was a kid he would walk down the aisle of the church and be "born again again" or "rededicate" his life to Christ every year at camp. In college he'd do it about every six months, then quarterly, and by the time he was in his forties it was about "four times a day."

As you become more aware of the condition of your soul, you must admit you're more angry than you want to be, or more selfish, or more afraid, or embarrassed, or prideful. Admitting it doesn't make you weak, it makes you honest. The more comfortable you become with confession, the more you will begin to practice it throughout the small moments of your day. When you do, you will begin to sense His grace throughout the small moments of your day, too. Confession is an opportunity to be reminded of your sinfulness, but more importantly, it's an opportunity to be reminded of God's grace and love for you.

In the next chapter you will learn a vocabulary to help you articulate what you are feeling, but for now, simply practice awareness and confession. Find a place to sit quietly, and pay attention to the stories and events that come to your mind and the way it makes you feel.

Let's end with a prayer and invite the Holy Spirit to help you be more aware of the condition of your soul, and His abiding presence in your life.

O Lord, meet me here.
I have nothing to bring You but
   my pride and insecurities,
   my craving for approval,
   and my fear of rejection.

Here, in this stillness,
   away from the world that always needs something from me;
Quiet my heart.
Quiet the sirens of worry, anxiety, and responsibility.
Give my mind reprieve from all of the tasks yet to be done
Teach me the truth about myself,
   and expose the lies that keep me from accepting Your love.

Let me be fully aware of Your presence
   and grace at work in my life.

Amen.

Chapter Summary

» Until you recognize what you're experiencing emotionally (your interior life), any attempts to *face your past*, *change your habits*, or *embrace your limits* will be hijacked by denial or naive optimism.

» Jesus was God as a human being. He had an interior life that reacted to his circumstances and surroundings. That means being more like Jesus requires becoming more human, not less.

» Being aware of how moments throughout your day affect you internally, and being able to articulate those feelings, helps you begin to fight against your deeply entrenched false self—the version of you that you believe God, and everyone else, needs you to be.

» Until you accept the truth about who you are, what you feel, and what you think, you will never expose your most vulnerable self to God.

» Confession is an opportunity to be reminded of your sinfulness, but more importantly, it's an opportunity to be reminded of God's grace and love for you.

CHAPTER FIVE

There's a Word for That

> "Spiritual transformation does not result from fixing our problems. It results from turning to God in the midst of them and meeting God just as we are. Turning to God is the core of prayer. Turning to God in our sin and shame is the heart of spiritual transformation."
> -David G. Benner

Study after study reveals we are more lonely, depressed, anxious, and addicted than ever before. But rarely will we admit it, because we don't know how we feel—or at least we don't know what to call it. While some people are adept at describing their emotions, most are not. We struggle to process or articulate our feelings because we lack the vocabulary—often resorting to describing our emotional state as simply "fine"—but having the language to name what you are experiencing is a crucial step to prayer and confession. The Psalmist declared, "Let all that I am praise the LORD; with my whole heart, I will praise his holy name." I'm certain he had more in mind than *fine*.

The ability to identify and name your emotions helps to stop the unhealthy habits and cycles that happen by default. This chapter will help you gain the awareness and vocabulary to articulate what is happening in your interior life. Until you put words to your internal experiences, you will feel powerless to change.

There are hundreds of emotions, each with variations, blends, and nuances, but researchers generally agree on seven primary emotions of the human experience. (See image 5.1) There are four negative emotions—fear, anger, sadness, and disgust; two positive emotions—joy and excitement; and one neutral emotion—surprise.*

Every day, you experience these feelings of fear, anger, sadness, disgust, joy, excitement, and surprise in some combination. This may be hard to believe if you don't think of yourself as an emotional person, but it's true.

Stop for a moment and think about your day yesterday. Before reading any further, try to identify moments when you felt afraid, angry, sad, disgusted, joyful, excited, or surprised.

If recognizing your emotions feels challenging, that's okay. It will get easier, I promise. One reason this exercise is challenging is because of shame.** As you were trying to identify when you felt afraid, or excited, or angry, shame was the little devil on your

---

* Surprise is classified as neutral because you can be surprised positively or negatively. Think of showing up to work and your boss firing you or giving you an unexpected promotion. Both things would be surprising.

** The number of primary emotions is debated. The consensus is either seven or eight, and shame is the difference in most cases—some lists classify it as a primary emotion and some classify it as secondary. I have not included shame in my list of primary emotions as I see it as a secondary emotion that keeps you from experiencing primary emotions.

Negative	Positive	Neutral
Fear	Joy	Surprise
Anger	Excitement	
Sadness		
Disgust		

Image 5.1

shoulder making you feel bad for feeling that way. Shame tells you that you're a bad person for being angry, you're silly for being excited, or you need to get over your fear. Shame is the emotion that makes you embarrassed for having feelings. The more you listen to shame, the more you will deny the truth about the condition of your soul.

But shame is not the only reason it's hard to recognize your feelings. Another reason is because your primary emotions disguise themselves in all sorts of other feelings—there are different degrees and variations to what you feel. Within your primary emotions are countless others all leading back to the primary seven. Yesterday your fear may have felt like nervousness, sadness may have felt like discouragement, and anger may have felt like jealousy.

Not That, But Kind of Like That

We tend to have stereotypical imagery in our mind for what each emotion looks like. Anger looks like someone yelling. Sadness looks like someone crying. Fear looks like someone hiding. Joy looks like someone laughing. But each of these is just one expression of that emotion. As you try to identify and articulate your feelings, it's helpful to think in broader terms. For example, think of anger as any feeling of injustice, which includes anytime you feel like something is unfair. Think of sadness as any feeling of loss, which includes anytime you miss something. Think of fear as anything that feels uncertain, which includes anytime you're worried about outcomes.

> Anger (injustice/unfairness)
> Fear (uncertainty)
> Sadness (loss)
> Disgust (immediate dislike)
> Joy (deep satisfaction)
> Excitement (thrill)
> Surprise (shock/amazement)

With these new, broader definitions of your primary emotions, think again about yesterday, and see if you can identify any additional moments when something felt unfair, uncertain, lost, satisfying, or unexpected.

I hope it was easier this time. When there was no coffee in the breakroom, you weren't just irritated, you were angry. When your children got on the bus to go to school, that momentary thought of "I hope they are okay" was fear. When no one listened to your idea in the staff meeting, you weren't just ignored, you felt invisible—you were sad. It's worth pointing out that identical experiences can create different emotions too. The lack of coffee could have made you feel surprised, the children getting on the bus could have made you feel sad, and being ignored in the meeting could have made you feel angry—or you might have even felt a combination of emotions. There is no one-size-fits-all to feelings. In the words of the Psalmist, we are "wonderfully complex."

With each recognition, shame will fight you. Shouldn't you be strong enough not to let something as silly as coffee make you angry? Why do you always have to be so sensitive when someone gives you feedback? Using words like anger, sadness, and fear can make you feel fragile, weak, and inadequate, but you're not; you're simply human.

Like learning any language, getting comfortable with naming your feelings takes time, and fluency is developed through practice. As long as your emotional vocabulary is limited to intimidating words like anger, sadness, fear, or joy, you will feel like you are being overly dramatic about the smaller experiences of your day, but as you learn the language, you will learn that anger, for example, can feel like any number of different emotions—some more substantial than others.

I've provided a list of words that may better explain the primary emotions you are feeling. (See image 5.2) This list is not exhaustive, but it's a great starting point to name what you feel. As you read the list, circle any of the words that feel more common than others.

I encourage you to keep a list of emotions with you wherever you spend time praying or journaling. Over time, naming emotions will become more natural, but as you are getting started it's probably most helpful to look back and review the previous days or weeks and find words on your list that resonate with your experiences. Eventually, you will recognize your emotions as you are experiencing

Angry	**Sad**
Offended	Lonely
Threatened	Uninterested
Frustrated	Inadequate
Defeated	Ashamed
Jealous	Depressed
Afraid	**Disgusted**
Confused	Resentful
Helpless	Shameful
Anxious	Bitter
Worried	Disappointed
Vulnerable	Horrified
Joyful	**Surprised**
Confident	Startled
Grateful	Overwhelmed
Peaceful	Confused
Excited	Amazed
Passionate	Shocked

Image 5.2

them in real time. For example, before you walk into a big meeting you will recognize your excitement, or fear, or insecurity. Or when someone makes a harsh comment, you will recognize you feel startled, threatened, or offended. As your self-awareness grows, you will be surprised how connected you feel to your inner self. You will know how you feel, and even better, you will know how to pray.

What You Feel First

On your journey for awareness and language, you will experience all the primary emotions, but based on your personality and God-given design, you'll tend to feel either anger, sadness, or fear first. This is why it can be helpful to use a personality profile tool to better understand yourself. My hero and mentor, Eugene Peterson, had a life rule to never take a personality test, because he felt they depersonalized the unique human experience. He has a point—you are more than a test result or a label—but there's also no denying that your motivation, emotional responses, and bad habits are pretty predictable based on the way you're wired, and this information can be helpful as you identify your vulnerabilities.

One personality tool many people find helpful in identifying their dominant emotion and initial reactions to the world is called the Enneagram. Unlike the classifications of other personality tools that are based on traits, the Enneagram focuses on the motivations and fatal flaws of each of the nine personality types.[***]

For example, I am an Enneagram 5. In general, that means I am motivated to observe and understand the world around me, and to preserve what feels like my limited resources. My initial emotion in most situations is fear, due to uncertainty and a desire to understand and predict outcomes, and my bad habit is to withdraw and withhold

---

[***] I've provided more details of each Enneagram type in Appendix B.

for the sake of self-preservation. I still experience anger and sadness, of course, but I almost always feel confusion or uncertainty first. Personality tools like the Enneagram help explain how different people can emotionally respond to the same event differently based on their makeup. For example, a tragic death might cause one person to initially be sad, another person to be angry, and another person to be afraid.

Let me give you a general summary of how you might initially feel based on your Enneagram personality type:

- » Types 8, 9, and 1 are all connected by their desire for justice. Because of this, their dominant negative emotion is anger. It is easier for them to see unfairness in the world, which provokes that anger inside of them.
- » Similarly, types 2, 3, and 4 are connected through empathy and social intelligence. Because of this, they are overly aware of their social standing at any given moment, and their dominant negative emotion is shame (an expression of sadness)—they desperately want to belong and measure up.
- » Lastly, types 5, 6, and 7 are connected by their craving for stability and security. Because of this, their dominant negative emotion is fear and anxiety. Searching for certainty can cause them to hyper-plan, or become indecisive.

It doesn't matter what tool you use; I use the Enneagram simply because it is the tool I am most familiar with. What's important is having the self-knowledge to know how you internally process your moment-by-moment life experiences.

Let's end this chapter with an exercise. Grab a piece of paper or a journal, and find a quiet place to reflect. On your piece of paper, write down four questions:

What am I angry about? (feels unfair)
What am I sad about? (feels like loss)
What am I anxious about? (feels uncertain)
What am I glad about? (feels like joy)

Don't be in a hurry. Take each question one at a time. As you sit in your quiet place, write down the answers that come to your mind. You may have a long or short list of answers—it doesn't matter. You may be angry about something that happened 20 years ago, or something that happened yesterday; just write it down. As I have helped people with this exercise I am always amazed at what experiences come to mind. I've had grown men with families of their own express anger about ways their father was absent in their life decades ago. I know from my own experiences that I began feeling deep sadness over my mother's death, which happened 10 years before I began asking, "What am I sad about?" Some days the answers will come from a deep place of suppression, but most days, this exercise allows you to simply reflect on recent moments and experiences, and name the feelings that you feel. They've been there all along, they are just waiting to be acknowledged.

Before you begin, pray the words of Psalm 139:13–16.

DEEP CHANGE

You made all the delicate, inner parts of my body
and knit me together in my mother's womb.
Thank you for making me so wonderfully complex!
Your workmanship is marvelous—how well I know it.
You watched me as I was being formed in utter seclusion,
as I was woven together in the dark of the womb.
You saw me before I was born.
Every day of my life was recorded in your book.
Every moment was laid out
before a single day had passed.

Chapter Summary

» The ability to identify and name your emotions helps to stop the unhealthy habits and cycles that happen by default.

» There are hundreds of emotions, each with variations, blends, and nuances, but researchers generally agree on seven primary emotions of the human experience. There are four negative emotions—fear, anger, sadness, and disgust; two positive emotions—joy and excitement; and one neutral emotion—surprise.

» We tend to have stereotypical imagery in our mind for what each emotion looks like. Anger looks like someone yelling. Sadness looks like someone crying. Fear looks like someone hiding. Joy looks like someone laughing. But each of these is just one expression of that emotion. As you try to identify and articulate your feelings, it's helpful to think in broader terms.

» Based on your personality and God-given design, you'll tend to feel either anger, sadness, or fear first.

CHAPTER SIX

The Language of Prayer

"We are most ourselves when we pray."
- **Eugene Peterson**

Everyone prays, kind of. It's an instinctual response. But the quality of interaction we long for often gets buried under the debris of the routines and distractions that keep us unaware of our true selves, and keep us praying about everything except the truth. As you begin to *feel your feelings*, the way you pray will be profoundly affected—specifically the words you say to God, when you say them, and the way you say them.

As you develop an awareness of and vocabulary for the experiences of your interior life, prayer becomes more relational and less transactional. There should be an ease to it—the kind of ease between close friends who can be silent or talk incessantly and it doesn't matter. At that level of ease, you stop praying because you *have* to, and instead begin to *want* to. I love the way Robert Mullholland defines prayer as a relationship with God "that becomes the context within which we experience all the events and relationships of our lives." This kind of prayer is a running dialogue between you and God for anything and everything that's happening; a moment-by-moment opportunity to involve God in your life. This is the kind of interaction our souls long for, the kind where God guides, instructs, and accompanies us as we attempt to live by faith—correcting our mistakes, steering our choices, forgiving our lapses, and encouraging our efforts. This is much different from making formal requests or repeating platitudes. Mullholland is describing prayer as an open-ended exchange between two people who are closely connected.

I am just barely old enough to remember a time when most people didn't have a cell phone, and the Internet was something you had to dial into. When my wife and I first started dating, I would call her house phone and ask her father if I could speak with his daughter. Crazy, I know. But now I'm raising a teenager, and I'm amazed at how she stays connected with her friends even when they are apart. The communication never ends; they simply pick up where they left off.

While constant connection to technology isn't healthy, it gives us a great picture of the kind of prayer that Mulholland is suggesting, and that the Apostle Paul described when he encouraged us to "pray without ceasing." It's possible to sense God's presence and grace moment by moment, not because you're lost in some trance-like state, but rather because you come to believe that every moment is holy, and that God is working and revealing Himself in even the most mundane or aggravating moments of your day. Do you believe that? Do you really believe it's possible to feel an intimate connection with God while you're folding laundry or making sales calls or sitting in traffic?

Tish Harrison Warren does a remarkable job describing this in her book *Liturgy of the Ordinary*. She says, "These moments are an opportunity for formation, for sanctification. Underneath these overreactions and aggravations lie true fears. My lost keys reveal my anxiety that I won't be able to do what I need to do to take care of myself and those around me. They hit on my fear of failure and incompetency. My broken dishwasher uncovers my worries about money—will we have enough to fix it? And it exposes my idolatry of ease, my false hope in comfort and convenience…"

Without an awareness or vocabulary for your internal reactions, the events of your day are just obligations or annoyances. But now, they are an invitation to experience the presence and grace of God wherever you are and whatever you're doing. God is working and moving even in—especially in—the most mundane moments and places.

One of my favorite stories in the Bible is an obscure passage about a seemingly normal day in between the spectacular days of the life of Abraham. He had just been caught in a lie, and was forced to leave Egypt, so he left and set up camp at a place between Bethel and Ai. I'm certain he was disappointed, confused, and battling feelings of failure, but it says that Abraham "worshiped the Lord *at that place* again."

We must never forget that faith is practiced in places—real places you can touch and feel. For a believer, these are sacred spaces—

holy ground. Faith is not an emotion we carry around with us, an aspirational set of ideals, or a memory of the glory days. No, faith is lived among real people, in real places, measured by seconds on a clock. This means that where you are standing is holy ground—a place where you can experience God. Yes, He is with you in the valley of the shadow of death, but He is also there while you pay bills, scrape marker stains off your walls, and try to get the lawnmower to start. He is talking to you, shaping and forming you, and inviting you to respond in kind. But how?

Find the Words

One day the disciples came to Jesus with a request: "Teach us how to pray." In response, Jesus didn't focus on techniques or advice. Instead, he gave them specific words to say, beginning with, "Our Father in heaven, hallowed be thy name." In this, Jesus was teaching a powerful lesson: the best way to learn how to pray is to learn the language from someone else who already knows it. Historically, these scripted prayers, hymns, and readings prayed at specific times are called *liturgy*.

Christians have been using the Psalms and liturgies written by the saints and poets to find a language for their prayer life for thousands of years. These prayers can be performed in large settings like worship services, but they can also be short, private prayers that help you say what you feel better than you could if you had to come up with the language on your own. It takes much of the pressure off of prayer because you don't have to come up with what to say; all you have to do is show up. As Pete Grieg says, "When your soul is spent and you've run out of imagination and initiative, it's a relief to be told what to say by someone you trust… being part of something very old—bigger than my own chaotic predicament and stronger than my own brittle resolve…" There is something relieving, something sedating about the predictability and routine. For example, I begin almost every morning by reciting Psalm 25, followed by this short prayer:

God, meet me this morning.

In the stillness and quiet
   of the start of a new day.
Before the world needs something from me
Before the sirens of worry,
   anxiety,
   and responsibility sound
Quiet my heart.

There is no pressure today.
If I succeed or if I fail,
   it doesn't change the way You
   see me,
   love me,
   or why You saved me.

I have nothing to prove
   only everything to receive

*Let me be fully aware of Your grace and limits
  at work in my life.*

Amen.

I recite the words of Psalm 25 because David begs God, "do not let me be disgraced," and that's one of my biggest fears in life—that I would be discredited or seen as illegitimate. I need the Psalmist's words to remember that "no one who ever trusts in you [God] will be disgraced" and that "honesty and integrity will protect me."

My fears of illegitimacy can cause me to begin each day striving for accomplishment and credibility—to feel the need to prove my worth—so I recite the words my soul needs so badly: "I have nothing to prove, only everything to receive."

This is just one example of how scripted prayers and worship patterns can be beneficial. I have a folder on my computer with liturgies for all kinds of scenarios, including battling feelings of failure, walking into a difficult meeting, being tired of waiting on God, and preparing to preach a sermon. Whenever I find a prayer that helps me articulate the language of my soul, I save it. The power of liturgy is in its consistency. There's no pressure to decide what to say or how long to say it, and you don't gauge its effectiveness by emotional response. You simply show up, be still, recite, and receive.

Those who grew up with less contemplative worship styles might worry that repeating or reciting words would lack a certain energy—wouldn't the routine and predictability become boring? It's possible. But really, anything can become predictable and boring. In the spirited Pentecostal worship services I grew up in, you could set your clock to the "spontaneous" moves of God, not because anyone was being disingenuous, but because we all, no matter what style, fall into predictable patterns of worship. This is true for an unhealthy emphasis on both extremes—contemplation and demonstration. Routine and predictability are not inherently bad things. The more spiritual depth and emotional health you develop, the more you will come to appreciate that something doesn't have to be spectacular to be spiritual. Many of the cornerstone practices of the Christian faith, like baptism and communion, have used the same patterns for centuries, because the power is in the practice.

Notice that this facet of relationship with God has very little to do with studying the Bible. There is an important time and place for that, and we will discuss it in the *Change Your Habits* practice, but being with God and learning about God are two very separate things. Many modern Christians primarily spend the majority of their "quiet time" reading or learning, and that is helpful, but in their efforts to learn, rarely do they view their "time with God" as an opportunity to simply be *with* Him. Learning about God is certainly vital to long-term spiritual maturity—faith without any facts is just superstition—but consider that Christians did not have personal copies of the Bible for roughly 1,400 years after Christianity began. Our modern focus on personally reading and studying the Bible would be a foreign concept to them. We must not forget that God wants a relationship with us, and relationship involves presence—being together.

When St. Benedict wrote about the monastic life in *The Rule of*

St. Benedict, he clearly separated worship from study. Seven times each day, the monks come together to sing the Psalms in worship and prayer, and also, at different times each day, have *lectio divina*, or "divine reading," for intellectual and spiritual development. Praying the scriptures, as opposed to just reading them, helps us develop what Eugene Peterson calls a "prayerful imagination." In this way, we look to the scriptures not primarily for information, but rather to be exposed and sharpened, to be human before God.

Whenever I teach about St. Benedict or the monastic life, someone always argues, "That's great for them, but I'm not a monk, and I don't have all day to sit in silence and pray." It's true that reading about our spiritual heroes can sometimes remind us of how their settings seemed uniquely optimized for spirituality, but have you ever considered that the same God who fills the halls of a monastery is with you while you fold laundry, exercise at the gym, or sit in the carpool line at your kid's school? Prayer is not only something we do at a reserved time and place when conditions are just right; it is an ongoing interaction between you and Him. You don't need a Bible, a podcast, or a devotional book—all you need to do is be *with* Him. What if you created a short liturgy for folding laundry and taped it to the bottom of your laundry basket? Just something to refocus your attention to the fact that you are completely and totally in the presence of a God who is pleased with you. Something like:

God,
I have many things to do today.
My mind is already overwhelmed by the tasks

and the limited time I have to complete them.
My responsibilities are not unimportant,
   but I am more than the things I do or how well I do them.
You are with me as I work.
At this very moment,
   while I perform this routine task,
   Your presence is here.
This is holy ground.

Amen.*

I'm not suggesting liturgy should be the only way you pray. The Bible encourages us to pray in and led by God's spirit, but as long as prayer is primarily about requests, it will remain transactional and superstitious. Dominican priest and theologian Herbert McCabe gave an honest critique of prayer when he said, "…you pray high-mindedly for big but distant things like peace in Northern Ireland or you pray that your aunt will get better from the flu—when in fact you do not much care about these things; perhaps you ought to, but you don't. And so your prayer is rapidly invaded by distractions arising from what you really do want—promotion at work, let us say. Distractions are nearly always your real wants breaking in on your prayer for edifying but bogus wants. If you are distracted, trace your distraction back to the real desires it comes from and pray about these."

It's only through honest confession that prayer becomes

---

* I've provided a few examples of short liturgies you can use for daily activities in Appendix C.

personal. Whatever you do, find a way to be honest with God and aware of His presence. It's important to remember, as you finish the *Feel Your Feelings* practice, that the purpose is not to be more focused on yourself. When you invite the Holy Spirit into your interior life, become more aware, and learn a vocabulary, there will be a season where you are paying more attention to yourself than normal, and that can feel selfish. But the end goal is to love God with all of your heart, soul, mind, and strength. You are focusing on yourself now so that you can finally be able to love God and others from a place of humility and honesty. Moving forward, when you interact with God and others, you won't have to mask your insecurities or magnify your strengths. Through prayer and confession you will begin to believe that God loves you in spite of your faults, and it's then, and only then, that you will learn to love others in spite of their faults too.

Chapter Summary

» As you begin to feel your feelings, the way you pray will be profoundly affected—specifically the words you say to God, when you say them, and the way you say them.

» It's possible to sense God's presence and grace moment by moment, not because you're lost in some trance-like state, but rather because you come to believe that every moment is holy, and that God is working and revealing Himself in even the most mundane or aggravating moments of your day.

» The best way to learn how to pray is to learn the language from someone else who already knows it. Historically, these scripted prayers, hymns, and readings prayed at specific times are called *liturgy*.

» Routine and predictability are not inherently bad things. The more spiritual depth and emotional health you develop, the more you will come to appreciate that something doesn't have to be spectacular to be spiritual.

PRACTICE #2

Face Your Past

CHAPTER SEVEN

Looking Back to Move Forward

"The child is in me still... and sometimes not so still."
- Fred (Mr.) Rogers

With the 72nd pick in the 1997 Major League Baseball draft, the St. Louis Cardinals selected 18-year-old Rick Ankiel from Port St. Lucie High School. From the moment Ankiel began pitching in the minor leagues, it was obvious he was the real deal. He broke a Single-A record many people believed would never be broken, pitching 17 consecutive innings without giving up a hit. The following year, Ankiel was named minor league pitcher of the year, with a 2.35 ERA.

By 2000, just 16 months after starting his first game in the minor leagues, he got the call up and became a major-league pitcher, quickly becoming the ace of the pitching staff. He was 20 years old, doing what he loved, and doing it better than almost anyone else on the planet.

On a perfect fall day in October, Ankiel was the Game 1 starter for the National League Division Series against the Atlanta Braves.

His counterpart that day was future Hall of Famer Greg Maddux. The entire baseball world was watching. It was the coming out party on a national stage for the 21-year-old, who was averaging more than a strikeout every inning he took the mound.

The game couldn't have started any better. The Cardinals scored six runs in the top of the first, giving Ankiel more than enough breathing room, and he retired the side in the first and second innings. In the top of the third, though, Ankiel threw a low pitch that got past the catcher and was recorded as a wild pitch. No big deal—it happens. Pitchers throw wild pitches all the time. But in that moment, with that single pitch, something changed for Ankiel, and he would never be the same.

After another wild pitch, the batter walked to first base. Ankiel threw an even wilder pitch to the next batter, nowhere near the plate, and from there it snowballed. You can watch the video online; it's excruciating. Two more wild pitches. Four walks. Four runs. Ankiel was taken out of the game before the inning was over.

After the game, he swore it was just a mechanical hiccup. "This is nothing," he told reporters gathered around his locker. "It will never happen again." But it did happen again.

The Cardinals won the series against the Braves, and Ankiel was scheduled to take the mound against the New York Mets in the second round of the playoffs. In the first inning, he threw five pitches to the backstop, one over the batter's head, and was pulled from the game. That's when he knew it—he had the yips. In the blink of an eye, he went from an invincible kid who blazed his way through the minors to someone who had no idea where the ball was going when it left his hand. And worse, he had no idea how to fix it.

The sports world was in shock. No one really knows where the yips come from. It's a radioactive topic that no one wants to discuss out of fear it's contagious. What everyone knew but didn't want to say out loud was that very few professional athletes ever recapture their dominance after the yips. What happened? And how could it happen to Rick Ankiel?

What most people didn't know was a few months earlier, before the start of the season, Ankiel stood in a courtroom in Fort Pierce, Florida, and watched as his father was sentenced to six years in prison for taking part in a marijuana and cocaine smuggling operation. Like so many, Ankiel's relationship with his father was complicated. Richard Ankiel taught his son how to pitch. There are pictures of father and son playing catch in the backyard when Rick was only 3 years old, and his dad coached him all the way through Little League.

When he wasn't on the ball field, though, things were much different. Rick grew up watching his dad abuse his mom. Richard would come home drunk, and his son would sit in his room and hear his mom scream for help. Baseball was a means of escape, a few hours to focus on something he loved, a chance to just be a kid, free from his insecurities and fears, and free from his suspicion that he was the person his dad must think he is. "Because otherwise why would he say that stuff to me? Why would he be so angry?" Ankiel wondered.

When the game was over, he would consider sneaking one of the bats home with him in case things got really bad again, but he never had the courage to fight back or call the cops on his dad. Now, as an adult, and a rising superstar in his sport, he stood in the gallery of the courtroom and watched the man he loved but despised walk away in handcuffs. For six months, the issue hung over Ankiel, threatening to throw his soaring career into disarray, but somehow he maintained a remarkable calm through it all—that is, until that first pitch got past the catcher and hit the backstop.

Ankiel later described what went through his mind when the pitch rolled past the catcher: "Millions and millions of people just saw you throw a wild pitch on national television." He thought about his family and friends watching the game. He thought about his hometown he had wanted to represent proudly. He thought about his teammates and his manager who trusted him enough to give a rookie the start in Game 1. He thought about all the people he was letting down, and he thought about all of it in the span of about three seconds. That's the thing about childhood wounds—they're not a problem until they're a problem, but then they're a *big* problem.

No one knows what caused Rick to throw that pitch to the backstop, including himself, but one thing he knew for certain was the road to recovery had to go through his childhood bedroom. He admitted, "The fights of my childhood against a drunken, raging father had tracked me into manhood, and now the villain was within me, restless and relentless and just out of reach."

Over the next several seasons, Ankiel tried to recapture his magical talent. Describing his attempt to find answers, he said, "One moment, I was a pitcher. The next, I was a patient. A project. A cautionary tale. A lab rat. A fairly miserable human being. I was, quite suddenly, my father's son." He used breathing exercises, therapy, and number games. He used and abandoned medications. In his memoir, he admits he drank vodka before some starts. But nothing helped. Ankiel admitted, "My whole life I'd carried a shield, forged from the belief of who I thought I should be. What a man should be. That is, impenetrable." But when that first wild pitch hit the backstop, he felt a crack in his armor for the first time in his life.

Four years later, on March 9, 2005, the same day he was supposed to start a spring training game in Jupiter, Florida, Rick Ankiel walked into manager Tony La Russa's office and said, "I quit."[*]

Dealing with Your Brokenness

As you begin to *feel your feelings*, and endeavor to become more like Jesus, it won't take long to encounter a significant problem—you are not starting from scratch. So many of the feelings you feel and the way you do or don't process those feelings were learned in adolescence. There is no blank canvas on which you can start your new life. Yes, your sins are forgiven, and you have the power inside of you to change, but in order to find wholeness, you will have to work through your brokenness. No matter how great or miserable you think your past was, brokenness is inevitable, because the people who influenced you—parents, teachers, coaches, pastors, and friends—are all broken people.

There's no use shutting your eyes and saying it doesn't exist,

---

[*] In an incredible show of resolve, Ankiel actually rebuilt his career as an outfielder after his manager suggested the idea. It's hard enough to be a professional baseball player, never mind change positions in the middle of your career, but that's what Ankiel did, and quite successfully.

and certainly nothing good comes from wallowing in it and saying there's nothing you can do about it. It must be confronted head on. There's no other way around it. But as you begin to face your past, you'll come to discover something beautiful and unexpected—the darkest, most painful places of your life are actually where you find the ingredients for wholeness.

In the next chapter, we will examine specifically your family of origin and the profound effect it has on you, but your past is more than just your family. It includes every interaction, habit, hurt, belief, affirmation, criticism, success, and failure that formed you into the person you are today. Not to mention sexual partners, abuses you suffered, and relational wounds. The romantic lie of our society is that we are all individuals, free to be who we want to be and make the choices we want to make. But what we think of as free will is largely an illusion. Much of the time, we are simply responding in the ways we were taught—or modeled—to respond. Deep change requires facing the parts of us that need changing, or at least acknowledging them, and that requires looking back in order to move forward.

I've found that this practice, more than any other, is the one Christians resist most. We've come to believe there is an amount of spiritual depth or committment that will cancel out the painful emotional work needed to truly change. This is why many of even the most passionate Christians are still unable to receive criticism, acknowledge the way they make people feel, engage in healthy confrontation, and accept the habits and tendencies everyone else can see but is afraid to bring up. Consider these examples:

» Steven is a good employee. He works hard, shows up on time, and rarely leaves early. He prides himself on following through with his tasks, and cooperating with his coworkers. But anytime someone offers constructive criticism of Steven's work, he becomes incredibly defensive and lashes out at them. Sometimes, in his anger, he will criticize them by pointing out something they could have done better, or in more passive aggressive ways, he will ignore them or give them the silent treatment. When anyone asks if he's okay, Steven will assure them he's fine, but everyone knows he's not. Steven has never acknowledged that he felt overly criticized and unappreciated as a child, and as an adult, he overreacts and distances himself from anyone he considers to be "against him." Everyone in the office has learned to keep their opinions to themselves and only offer generally positive feedback to avoid upsetting Steven.

» Carl and Rebecca attended their last church for more than 10 years. They dedicated their children there and had become friends with the pastor and many other families in the church. The pastor had recently been busier than normal trying to finish the church building project, and Carl and Rebecca felt like they were being ignored. Instead of communicating how they felt to the pastor, they talked to other families in the church about how "the church isn't like it used to be," and, "the pastor is just too busy to care about the people anymore." They decided to leave the church, and convinced two other couples from their small group to go with them. When the pastor asked why they were leaving, they never answered honestly, and instead spoke only in generalities. Carl and Rebecca have never acknowledged that they grew up in religious environments where keeping the peace was prioritized over honest communication. So they harbor a lot of hurt feelings and bitterness toward people, but never bring it up.

» Stacy has always been a go-getter. She was a star athlete in high school, led her sorority in college, and after graduating, quickly climbed the ranks at a marketing firm. In her enthusiasm and drive to be successful, Stacy sometimes comes across as overly aggressive and makes her friends and coworkers feel intimidated. Occasionally someone will bring it up and let Stacy know that she hurt their feelings, or that she may be pushing a little too hard, but Stacy is always able to justify her behavior by saying, "they're just being too sensitive," or "I'm trying to get the best out of everyone." She has never recognized how much of her self-worth comes from being perceived as powerful, ambitious, and in charge. After a lifetime of affirmation for being strong, she doesn't recognize that her strength sometimes causes those around her to feel weak and unimportant.

These are just a few of many examples of how feelings, achievements, and messages from your past subconsciously affect your day-to-day life as an adult. Scientifically, we know that our formative years impact us for the rest of our lives. The years of our childhood shape and frame how we see the world and have deep, long-term ramifications. It's easy to jokingly assume that every counselor or therapist wants to talk about your relationship with your parents, but the truth is, every aspect of our self-worth, personality, coping mechanisms, core motivations, problem-solving responses, and what we believe to be normal, are *all* directly connected to what happened in our past. That means the way you react to someone rejecting you, someone criticizing you, or even someone trying to love you or care for you are reactions that you learned or saw modeled in your earliest years, and it shows up everywhere all the time. You struggle to celebrate instead of being jealous. You stay silent instead of honestly communicating how you feel. You explode in anger over seemingly small offenses. Why? Where did these emotions and reactions come from, and why isn't everyone else as bothered as you are? It's easy to blame your anxiety, worry, jealousy, anger, or other issues on your surroundings or circumstances, telling yourself, "It's not me, it was just a random moment of weakness." In reality, it is you. But it's not the adult version of you, it's the 7-year-old living inside you. The kid who won the trophies or got cut from the team, or who was hurt by Mom and Dad, or got passed over for the solo, or who got good grades or underachieved.

I read recently about the Europa, a hotel in Ireland that earned the nickname, "the most bombed hotel in the world." The Europa opened its doors in June of 1971 against a backdrop of rising political violence in Northern Ireland. During the first three years of its existence, the Europa was damaged by bombs 20 times—and a permanent notice was attached to each bedroom door warning guests to be prepared for a speedy evacuation from the building. An employee recalled the windows being blown out on a weekly basis. Between 1991 and 1993, there were 250 bomb warnings, and in its history, the building was damaged by explosions 33 times, but the Europa kept going, housing politicians, prime ministers, musicians, and movie stars, including Bob Dylan, Brad Pitt, Julia Roberts, and U2. The owners were determined that the hotel would not close its doors, so after each explosion, the staff swept up the debris, replaced the windows, and carried on. Incredibly, no one was killed by the attacks in the entire history of the hotel.

The story of the Europa is the perfect example of the way many of us try to sweep away the pain and trauma of our past experiences in an effort to continue on with business as usual. Clean up. Move on. Keep things moving. In some ways, this is necessary. Our brains are built to help us block out traumatic experiences that debilitate us. But unfortunately, the same ability that protects us also keeps us from finding freedom and healing from our past experiences. After decades of carrying on, we become masters of self-deception and never recognize the truth about why we are how we are.

Your journey toward deep change must go through your childhood bedroom, hometown, and high school hallways—from harmless habits to deeply destructive events like abuse or neglect. We all have people we need to forgive, traits we need to acknowledge, habits we need to change, and hurts we need to address. You cannot hope to escape your past by ignoring or denying its impact on you. There's much about yourself that you cannot change, like your height, your age, or your place of birth. At best, you can make modifications to your body and emotional temperaments. But even with so much out of your control, you are not stuck with your life the way it is. You can change—can be changed. "That is the promise of God in Jesus Christ and the experience that is at the heart of Christian living—*conversion*."

The purpose of facing your past is not to go back and right every wrong or dig up every skeleton. Nor is it to place blame. You made a mistake. You missed an opportunity. Someone lied to you or let you down. But guilt and blame only drain more energy out of you. The purpose of facing your past is simply to face it. Acknowledge its power and influence on your life. As you do, you will find the Holy Spirit there with you every step of the way, not only to make it possible to pursue wholeness, but also to deal with brokenness.

As you end this chapter and begin to face your past, pray the classic serenity prayer.

God grant me the serenity to accept the things I cannot change,
courage to change the things I can,
and wisdom to know the difference.

Amen.

Chapter Summary

» So many of the feelings you feel and the way you do or don't process those feelings were learned in adolescence.

» There is no blank canvas on which you can start your new life. Yes, your sins are forgiven, and you have the power inside of you to create a new life, but in order to find wholeness, you will have to work through your brokenness.

» Your past is more than just your family. It includes every interaction, habit, hurt, belief, affirmation, criticism, success, and failure that formed you into the person you are today. Not to mention sexual partners, abuses you suffered, and relational wounds.

» The purpose of facing your past is not to go back and right every wrong or dig up every skeleton. Nor is it to place blame. The purpose of facing your past is simply to face it. Acknowledge its power and influence on your life.

CHAPTER EIGHT

Family of Origin

> "Sometimes father and I were living together, sometimes I was with strangers and only saw him from time to time. People came into our lives and went out of our lives. We had now one set of friends, now another. Things were always changing. I accepted it all. Why should it ever have occurred to me that nobody else lived like that? To me, it seemed as natural as the variations of the weather and the seasons."
> -**Thomas Merton** *The Seven Storey Mountain*

How much do you trust your memory? Think for a moment about your honeymoon, or the day your child was born, or a game you won in high school. What do you remember? You might be surprised to discover that your memory is misleading. Psychologists call it *duration neglect*—it's when you recall an experience and focus only on the highest and lowest moments.

In their book, *The Power of Moments*, Chip and Dan Heath use a hypothetical family vacation to Disney World to help explain duration neglect. Imagine I texted you every hour during your trip, asking you to rate your experience at that exact moment on a scale from 1 to 10, 1 being lousy and 10 being terrific. Your answers might be as follows:

9 AM: Trying to dress your kids, feed them breakfast, and get everyone out of the hotel room. There's excitement in the air. **Rating: 6**

10 AM: Standing in a long line to ride It's A Small World together. **Rating: 5**

11 AM: Just finished riding the Space Mountain roller coaster. Your kids are begging to ride it again. **Rating: 10**

Noon: Spending way too much money on park food, but you were hungry. **Rating: 7**

1 PM: Waiting in more lines in the Florida heat. Kids are whining. **Rating: 3**

2 PM: Buying mouse ear hats as you leave the park. Your kids are adorable. **Rating: 8**

If we wanted to estimate how enjoyable your day was, we could simply average the ratings together, and arrive at the conclusion that it was a pretty good day: **6.5**. But what if we asked you to rate your overall experience a few weeks later? You would assume the answer is around 6.5, right? Wrong. Psychologists would guess that's way off! They predict that looking back on the day at Disney, your overall rating would be a 9! That's because research has found that in recalling an experience, we ignore most of what happened and focus instead on the very best or very worst moments. In your case, a few weeks after your trip you will predominantly remember riding Space Mountain **(10)** and buying mouse ear hats **(8)**. In a few years you will tell everyone, "We had the best time!" **(9)**

It's not only true for vacations, though—duration neglect shows up in many of our life experiences. When alumni were asked about their memories from college, 40% of their memories were from the month of September, when they were just arriving. It's true for low moments too. When colonoscopy patients were asked to recall their procedure, they retold the most painful moments. When we recall memories, we don't remember the average of our minute-by-minute or week-by-week experiences, we mostly remember the best and the worst of times.

What does duration neglect have to do with *facing your past*? Generally speaking, when we think about our childhood experiences, we tend to overestimate or underestimate how they shape our life— our happiest memories probably weren't quite as picture perfect as we remember, and our worst experiences probably weren't as intolerable as we recall. In order to experience deep change and be the person God wants us to be, we must go back and understand how our family of origin shaped our desires, beliefs, and actions. Yes, you are a Christian following the ways of Jesus, but unconsciously you still follow the tendencies and patterns of your family.

If we were to track your actions, thoughts, desires, feelings, and reactions for a day or a week, and do the same for the people who lived in the house you were raised in, most of those feelings and actions would be very similar. Sadly, when we look deep beneath the surface of our lives, most of us are not doing anything fundamentally different from what our families did. The good news is every Christian belongs to a new family—the family of God! We don't have to be defined by our family of origin, but we do have to be aware of it.

The Impact of Family

The Bible is filled with stories about families, and it has a lot to say. When you see the word "family" in the Bible, it's referring to your entire extended family over three to four generations—this includes all your brothers, sisters, uncles, aunts, grandparents, great-grandparents, and significant others going back almost 150 years. In some large ways, and many small ways, the blessings and sins of your family going back two to three generations profoundly impact the person you are today.

When giving Moses the Ten Commandments, God said, "...for I, the LORD your God, am a jealous God, punishing the children for the sin of the fathers to the third and fourth generation of those who hate me, but showing love to a thousand generations of those who love me and keep my commandments."

At first glance, this seems harsh. The idea of punishing future generations for the sins of their ancestors doesn't seem fair. But the original Hebrew word used for "punish" in this verse is *paqad*, and it means "consequences that repeat," or "consequences becoming fully known." With that understanding, we can read God's message to

Moses differently. The meaning is that the sins of one generation *tend to repeat themselves* or *the consequences become fully known over three to four generations.*

As you think about your experiences and the tragic stories you've heard about alcohol, adultery, divorce, addictive behavior, sibling rivalry, sexual abuse, conflict, crime, and more, you may notice that many of these behaviors are patterns that can be seen repeated over multiple generations of a family. The opposite is also true—blessings tend to repeat and reveal themselves generationally too.

Why does any of this matter? Why can't we just move on with our lives, let the past be the past, and forget about it, or at least ignore it? While it feels like it would be easier to ignore the painful and unhealthy parts of our past, facing them is crucial because we have been shaped by those experiences.

God's desire for us to leave behind our sinful family patterns is similar to the desire He had for the Israelites to leave Egypt. Although the Israelites did physically leave the land of Egypt, a great deal of Egyptian culture and thinking remained in them. In the same way, we may leave home, but we continue to unconsciously follow the "rules" we internalized in our families of origin.

Your family's influence over your life begins long before you ever realize it. According to research, children as young as 18 months can determine what their mother values by following the gaze of her eyes. When a mother looks at something, "a baby takes that as a signal that the mother desires the object, or is at least paying attention to it because it must be important." It's not long before the baby can follow not just her mother's eyes, but even the intentions behind her actions. You start wanting things long before you can articulate why you want them, and this in large part was shaped by watching what was important to the people who raised you.

For example, my dad was a preacher, and his dad was a preacher, and his dad was a preacher. That's three generations of men who stood on stages and preached to congregations. In fact, most of my uncles are preachers, too. Even though no one ever told me I had to be or should be a preacher myself, I subconsciously assigned a certain value to preaching from an early age because all the men in my life who I loved and respected were preachers. Thankfully, I was blessed with a model of amazing spiritual leadership in my childhood—I can think of a lot worse models to follow—but that doesn't mean that even something positive like preaching didn't impact my life in negative ways too. By performing on stages and being in front of crowds from an early age, I learned to overvalue the applause and approval of people, I struggle to feel comfortable in my own skin when I'm in smaller settings, and I battle insecurity when I'm around other men who are more skilled in physical activity than me. This is a personal example of how even something as positive as a legacy of strong Christian men can still impact you negatively. This is not because anyone intended to pass down negative qualities, but because our sinful natures can take even the best things and make them unhealthy.

It's important to remember there is no such thing as a perfect family. No matter how good or bad your family experience was, you picked up certain unhealthy traits and values that contradict God's plan for you. This doesn't mean you should go back and try to rewrite a good childhood into a bad one. It just means that having loving parents, or money, or living in a good neighborhood doesn't exempt you from habits and wounds that make it hard to be more like Jesus. It also means that if you view your childhood as extremely unhealthy, you should not assume that others were much more fortunate than you. Of course, certain challenges are more severe than others, but comparing your situation to another can cause an unfair or dishonest representation of a person's need for grace. The sooner you can let go of your ideal image of childhood, the sooner you'll be able to heal from the past that hurt you. Most parents did the best they could with what they brought with them into adulthood. And "it is often the case that some of the things that did hurt us, such as criticism and rejection, were a result of what was handed to them by their families of origin, rather than a reflection on us or their love for us."

Our first instinct when broaching the subject of past wounds may be to feel shame or anger toward our families, but instead we must embrace the fact that God chose to bring us into a particular family, in a particular place, at a particular moment in history, and He does not make mistakes. Your family of origin provided you with certain opportunities and gifts, but it also handed you certain hurts, habits, and harmful ideas that you carried with you into adulthood. Unfortunately, it is not possible to erase these negative effects. Family history lives inside all of us, especially in those who attempt to bury it, but only the truth will set you free.

Think about some of the well-known families in the Bible and the sinful patterns that repeated themselves:

» Abraham was an incredible example of faith, but under pressure, he reverted to being dishonest. His son, Isaac, lied in almost exactly the same way his father did, and Isaac's son, Jacob, was known as a deceiver who lied to his dying dad, his brother, and his father-in-law.

» David was a faithful shepherd and highly skilled musician, but he grew up as the youngest son in a family of sibling rivalry. David's kids also lived with intense feelings of rivalry, including murder, sexual abuse, and one of the sons trying to kill his dad.

While your family history may not include murder, if we look closely enough, we can all find qualities we are not proud of, and even worse, we can see those very qualities in ourselves. Still, God did not disqualify Abraham and David, and He does not disqualify you and me. Even the worst, most painful, most embarrassing parts of our past can be used by God for something beautiful.

Your Origin Story

As you begin to face the behaviors and beliefs found in your family of origin, pray that the Holy Spirit will help you recognize things that were previously unknown, and accept the impact they have on you. Consider things like: what pressure did you feel being a part of your family? What were the "scripts" or unwritten life rules your family lived by? What values were most celebrated, and what flaws were most villainized?

In *Emotionally Healthy Spirituality*, Peter Scazzero lists "10 Family Commandments" to help you examine some of the spoken and unspoken behavioral patterns in your childhood home.

How did your family deal/interact with the following issues:
1. Money
2. Conflict
3. Sex
4. Grief and loss
5. Expressing anger
6. Family
7. Relationships
8. Attitudes toward other cultures
9. Success
10. Feelings and emotions

This practice can take some time. Don't be frustrated if it takes longer than you'd like. When you are ready, I want to encourage you to write an Origin Story. It can be as long or as short as you want it to be—what's important is to articulate what values, habits, and hurts your family of origin gave you, and more importantly, how Jesus is changing you.

There's no right or wrong way to do it, but I've provided a template to help you get started:

I grew up in a home/family that **(write as many descriptions about your family as you want).** *This caused me to* **(describe**

your instinctual responses/beliefs/actions). *But Jesus is teaching me that* **(write all the ways the truth, Jesus, and the family of God are making you a new person).**

It's always a powerful and emotional moment when someone reads their origin story. I have provided a few examples from friends of mine to help you begin to write your own.

» I grew up in a well-known family that was considered a prominent part of society. No matter what, family was the most important thing. If you weren't for us, you were against us. I learned early that being strong, dominant, and self-sufficient was celebrated, so I worked hard to be an independent woman. But as an adult, I began to notice how my self-reliance made it really hard to connect with and rely on others. Jesus is helping me learn that vulnerability isn't weakness, and that He doesn't need me to be strong for Him. As a matter of fact, His strength is made perfect in my weakness.

» I grew up in a loving yet broken home. My mother lived in our home, but I was raised by my grandparents. My mom seemed to care more about herself than me, and my dad did not want a relationship with me. From an early age I wanted to be the complete opposite of my mother. I wanted to feel loved and seen. I wanted to feel like I was worthy of happiness. I idolized the God-centered marriage my grandparents had and believed a marriage like theirs would make me happy and whole. When

I got married, I put too much pressure on my husband, which almost ended up destroying our family. I was broken, hurt, and expecting my husband to complete all the broken parts of me. When he messed up, or didn't do things the way I wanted them done, it always left me disappointed in not only him, but myself, because I did not feel that I could ever measure up to be enough in someone's eyes. Jesus is helping me to recognize my worth is not in who I am or how other people view me; my worth comes from what He did for me on the cross. I am made new because Jesus gave His life so that I could have mine, and I intend to live this new life to the fullest.

» I grew up in a family that was completely broken relationally. My parents' marriage was devoid of intimacy, shared experiences, or conversation. My father preferred to be by himself and lived independently of my mom, me, and my sister. He rarely came to events or sports that my sister and I were involved in, and often would leave a room if we were all there or got too loud. It made me feel very alone and caused me to keep my thoughts and feelings to myself and not depend on others to solve problems or figure out how to move through life, and thus made relationships very difficult. Because my father gave the impression of not wanting to be with us, I worked hard to gain his approval through intelligence and athleticism, and my worth and value were dependent on whether he noticed me or affirmed something I did. Over the years, I have given men in my life this same power, gaining my value and worth through their approval.

Jesus is teaching me that from the moment I get up until I fall asleep, He is pleased with me—all I can do is the best I can do and the outcomes belong to Him. My value and worth aren't based on anything I do, but instead what He did on the cross.

» I grew up in a home where my dad was in charge, and I feared him. My mom babied me, so naturally I created a strong bond with her and a distant relationship with my dad. My mom always made me feel special, and prioritized my needs over her own and my dad's. This made me more selfish, and as I became a husband and a father, I struggled to adjust to not being the center of attention and not always getting my way. Jesus is helping me learn that true joy is found in loving others, and that I don't have to always have my way. He's also helping develop a deeper relationship with my dad later in life.

You may not be ready to write your origin story yet. That's okay. Just begin by answering some of the questions presented in this chapter. Let's end by praying and asking God to help us on this incredibly personal and courageous journey.

God, You placed me into my particular family
  in a particular place
  in a particular time in history.

I don't see what You see,
  but I know Your ways are higher than mine.
Help me to see the purposes in Your plan.

DEEP CHANGE

Lord, I do not want to betray
  or be ungrateful for what was given to me.
But at the same time,
I do not want to be held prisoner by my past.
Help me see what I need to let go of.
Help me face issues that must be addressed.

Grant me courage and wisdom;
  to learn from the past
  but not be crippled by it.

Amen.

Chapter Summary

» In order to experience deep change and be the person God wants us to be, we must go back and understand how our family of origin shaped our desires, beliefs, and actions.

» When you see the word "family" in the Bible, it's referring to your entire extended family over three to four generations—this includes all your brothers, sisters, uncles, aunts, grandparents, great-grandparents, and significant others going back almost 150 years.

» The original Hebrew word used for "punish" in Exodus 20:4–6 is *paqad*, and it means "consequences that repeat," or "consequences becoming fully known." The meaning is that the sins of one generation *tend to repeat themselves* or *the consequences become fully known over three to four generations.*

» Our first instinct when broaching the subject of past wounds may be to feel shame or anger toward our families, but instead we must embrace the fact that God chose to bring us into a particular family, in a particular place, at a particular moment in history, and He does not make mistakes.

CHAPTER NINE

The Story of Pain

"How shalt thou hope for mercy, rendering none?"
-The Duke of Venice *The Merchant of Venice*

As you begin to face your past, you will no doubt unearth emotions and hurts that you would much rather avoid. We all have them—the defining, sometimes traumatic, moments that still hold us hostage decades later. It's the man who is struggling to be a father because he's never been able to forgive his own father. It's the wife who cannot look past her husband's faults because her mother did the same to her. It's the person who can't find it in them to love again after a stinging betrayal. What all the stories have in common is a wounded person waiting for something or someone to make it right, but atonement rarely, if ever, occurs.

Deep change requires that you make peace with your most painful wounds, because those wounds shape your deeply-held beliefs—the narratives you have told yourself over and over to make sense of your hurt. After repeating it enough times, you perfect the story of pain, perfectly casting the villains and the victims. You master your tone in the storytelling, and you bring those stories with you into every new relationship. Think about the prayer requests and stories shared in your small group or the conversations shared around the Thanksgiving table—they are *the* stories that define us, but in all your retelling, have you ever come to any different conclusions? Or have you simply assigned straightforward explanations to complex human problems?

While we say we would love to move on or get past it, it's not that simple. In some ways, our stories have become our identity. You are the woman who was cheated on, or the employee who was treated unfairly. You are the business partner who was stolen from, or the kid who was neglected. In ways we may not recognize or want to admit, our anger becomes a source of energy. If we were able to let it go, what would we talk about? Who would we be? Frederick Buechner accurately described this when he said, "Of the Seven Deadly Sins, anger is possibly the most fun. To lick your wounds, to smack your lips over grievances long past, to roll over your tongue the prospect of bitter confrontations still to come, to savor to the last toothsome morsel both the pain you are given and the pain you are giving back—in many ways it is a feast fit for a king. The chief drawback is that what you are wolfing down is yourself. The skeleton at the feast is you." This echoes St. Augustine's argument that envy and hatred try to pierce our neighbor with a sword, when the blade cannot reach him unless it first passes through our own body.

Forgiveness and healing are so vital to spiritual depth and

emotional health that Jesus instructed his disciples to halt worship in pursuit of reconciliation. That may include actual resolution in some instances, but in most cases, it's about the psychological release of refusing to be defined by your suffering. This is easier said than done, of course. We struggle to forgive. We hope the person who wronged us will feel just an ounce of the pain we've experienced because of what they've done to us, and we can't let go until we feel pain has been fairly distributed. But in most instances, our anger is directed at a ghost. Our offender is real, but they are rarely the character we have recreated in our mind, and they often have no way of understanding how much hurt they've caused us.

There's an old taoist parable about a young farmer who was covered with sweat as he paddled his boat upstream to deliver his produce to the village. It was a hot day and he was hurrying to get home before dark. As he looked ahead, he saw another vessel heading rapidly downstream toward his boat. This vessel seemed to be making every effort to hit him, so he rowed furiously to get out of the way, but it didn't seem to help.

He yelled at the other vessel, "Change direction, you idiot! You are going to hit me. The river is wide. Be careful!" His screaming was to no avail. The other vessel hit his boat with a sickening thud. He was enraged as he stood up and cried out to the other vessel, "You moron! How could you manage to hit my boat in the middle of this wide river? What's wrong with you?"

As he looked at the other boat, he realized there was no one in it. He was screaming at an empty vessel that had broken free of its moorings and was going downstream with the current.

The lesson is simple: There is never anyone in the other boat. In almost every case, the greater danger than what happened to you is how you will remember, explain, and retell what happened to you. "Myth becomes myth in the retelling."

Choosing to Forgive

In his book, *What's So Amazing About Grace?*, Philip Yancey shares a remarkable story about a woman named Rebecca who married a pastor. In time, it became obvious to Rebecca that her husband had a dark side. He dabbled in pornography, and solicited escorts on his trips to other cities. Sometimes he asked Rebecca for forgiveness, and sometimes he did not. He eventually left her for another woman named Julianne.

Rebecca shared how painful it was for her, a pastor's wife, to suffer this humiliation. Some church members who respected her husband treated her as if the infidelity had been her fault. Devastated, she found herself pulling away from human contact, unable to trust people. She could never put her husband out of mind, because they had children, so she had to make regular contact with him in order to arrange visitation.

Rebecca had the increasing sense that unless she forgave her former husband, a hard lump of revenge would be passed on to their children. She prayed for months. At first, her prayers seemed as vengeful as some of the Psalms—she asked God to give her ex-husband "what he deserved." Finally, she came to the place of letting God, not herself, determine "what he deserved."

One night, Rebecca called her ex-husband and said, in a shaky, strained voice, "I want you to know that I forgive you for what you've done to me. And I forgive Julianne too." He laughed off her apology, unwilling to admit he had done anything wrong. Despite his rebuff, that conversation helped Rebecca get past her bitter feelings.

A few years later, Rebecca got a frenzied phone call from Julianne. She had been attending a ministerial conference with her husband in Minneapolis, and he had left the hotel room to go for a walk. A few hours passed, then Julianne heard from the police—he had been arrested for soliciting sex.

On the phone with Rebecca, Julianne was sobbing. "I never believed you," she said. "I kept telling myself that even if what you said was true, he had changed. And now this. I feel so ashamed, and hurt, and guilty. I have no one on earth who can understand. Then I remembered the night you said you forgave us. I thought maybe you could understand what I'm going through. It's a terrible thing to ask, I know, but could I come talk to you?" Somehow, Rebecca found the courage to invite Julianne over. They sat in her living room, cried together, shared stories of betrayal, and prayed together. Julianne now points to that night as the time when she became a Christian.

When we read stories like Rebecca's, we so badly want to do the same. We want to be able to forgive the people who hurt us or let us down. We want to move on and live in freedom, but we just can't do it. When you've been wronged, you can contrive a hundred reasons against forgiveness. They need to learn a lesson. You don't want to encourage irresponsible behavior. They need to learn that actions have consequences. "It's not up to me to make the first move." "How can I forgive them if they're not even sorry?" When seen as just mushy sentiment, forgiveness feels like turning a blind eye for the greater good—as if you should minimize your hurt to keep the peace—but that is not what Jesus teaches. He never pressures you to condone, excuse, deny, minimize, or forget the wrong. What happened to you was wrong. Instead, Jesus teaches that forgiveness is a freely-made choice to give up revenge, resentment, or harsh judgments toward a person who caused the hurt, and strive to respond with generosity, compassion, and kindness toward that person.

We marvel at those who are able to make this choice. Martin Luther King Jr. wrote about his excruciating journey of forgiveness from the Birmingham City Jail while Southern pastors stood outside with mobs yelling for him to be hanged and policemen swung nightsticks at his unarmed supporters. After the Civil War, politicians and advisers urged Abraham Lincoln to punish the South severely for all the bloodshed it had caused, but Lincoln refused, saying, "Do I not destroy my enemies when I make them my friends?" In these examples we do not find a sentimentalism, but instead a hard logic and reasoning that forgiveness is the responsibility of the offended, not the offender.

Forgiveness offers a way out. It does not settle all questions of blame and fairness. To be clear, forgiveness *is* unfair, but it is the only way to a fresh start—a new beginning. This is so important that when the disciples asked Jesus to teach them how to pray, He included the words, "Forgive us our trespasses as we forgive those who trespass against us." Of all the things Jesus could have instructed us to include in our prayers, He made sure to include forgiveness. Why? Because it is fundamental to the Christian life—*you have been forgiven an infinite debt*. A Christian who can't forgive does not yet understand forgiveness. They still believe debts have to be repaid. They cannot give grace because they do not yet believe they have actually received it. But Jesus wanted part of our daily rhythm to include a reminder of our wrongs and His mercy, so it would be fresh in our minds and so we could extend the same grace we have received.

Hurt People Hurt People

But there is one more painful truth about forgiveness we must confront—another lesson from Jesus' life. On the evening of His crucifixion, while hanging on the cross and just a few hours from death, He looked down and saw the same people who claimed to love Him but had instead voted to kill Him. In those moments, Jesus had the supernatural ability to take action. No one in history had more capability to get even with his enemies than Jesus. The options were endless! He could have called down lightning to strike them, or poisoned their water, or damned them to Hell, but instead of taking recourse, He chose to pray to the Father on their behalf and forgive them. And in His prayer, He gave you and me the secret to offering forgiveness when it seems impossible to give. He said, "Father, forgive them, for they don't know what they are doing."

With those seven words, "they don't know what they are doing," Jesus gives us the most compelling reason to forgive: *pity*. Not a condescending disdain, but real pity that feels sorrow and compassion because of the suffering of others. I'm sure there is a small percentage of people in the world who are terrible, hateful, despicable human beings, and they hurt people on purpose for the fun of it, but I've never met one. In all my years, I've just met lots of hurt people who hurt people. It's not an excuse or justification for their actions, but it is an acceptance of the fact that the people who hurt us did not truly know what they were doing. Yes, the dad who walked out on you knows he hurt you, but he has no idea how badly he hurt you. The mom who never made you feel good enough knows she could have done better, but she has no idea how terribly she paralyzed you. The friend who betrayed you, the spouse who cheated on you, the kid who won't talk to you—*they don't know what they are doing*.

As long as your wounds cause you to feel superior, you'll never be able to forgive your offender. Every time you characterize them in your mind, you take away their humanity, making it that much easier to only see them as the worst thing they've ever done. In these moments, you are the person Jesus described, who has been forgiven of a debt far greater than you are owed, but in your hurt, you can't imagine a debt any greater than what is owed to you.

There was a time years ago when several leaders left our church, and over the next few months, many families followed them. It was a painful time for me and my family. We dealt with feelings of betrayal and anger, and for several years I retold stories I had perfected that allowed me to characterize the people who had left. I masterfully made them the villain and myself the victim, and it helped initially, as I felt justified in my anger, and my stories helped me bond with other wounded people. But eventually, all I had to show for my hurt was cynicism and hate.

After a few years, I had a good friend interrupt me as I was retelling the story of what had happened to me, and he said, "Jason, I want you to know I love you, and we can talk about what those people did to you for the rest of your life if you want to. I will be here for you. But I just want you to know, in case you don't recognize it, that this is all you really talk about anymore."

I sat there in my friend's car in a kind of daze. I was offended at first, but somewhere deep down, I knew he was right. The truth is I didn't realize how much I was talking about it. I didn't want to be that person. I desperately wanted to move past my pain.

A few weeks later, my wife and kids were out of town for a few days, so while I was alone I wrote a three-page letter to the people who I believed had done me wrong. I tried to explain how badly they had hurt me, but even as I wrote the letter I had to admit they didn't intend to impact me the way they did. There was no master plan or conspiracy to hijack two years of my life. They were just hurt, and in their pain, they had hurt me too. After I finished, I took the letter to my backyard and lit it on fire. I prayed and asked God to help me move on and never bring it up again.

I'm not suggesting my hurt is as bad as or worse than what you've experienced—I can't imagine the horrors done to you by people who claimed to love you. But I do know that spiritual depth and emotional health will never replace your hurt and bitterness until you make the choice to forgive and heal—and that choice is only yours to make.

What if today, with God's help, you made the same decision Jesus did hanging on the cross? Would you consider praying on behalf of your offender, "God, forgive _____ for _____. I believe they didn't know what they were doing, and even if they did know, they don't know how badly they've hurt me." You may choose to tell them, or they may never know, but forgiveness is your responsibility, not theirs, and freedom is yours to have if you're willing to take it.

Chapter Summary

» Deep change requires that you make peace with your most painful wounds, because those wounds shape your deeply-held beliefs—the narratives you have told yourself over and over to make sense of your hurt.

» Forgiveness and healing are so vital to spiritual depth and emotional health that Jesus instructed his disciples to halt worship in pursuit of reconciliation.

» A Christian who can't forgive does not yet understand forgiveness. They still believe debts have to be repaid. They cannot give grace because they do not yet believe they have actually received it.

» Jesus gives us the most compelling reason to forgive: *pity*. Not a condescending disdain, but real pity that feels sorrow and compassion because of the suffering of others. As long as your wounds cause you to feel superior, you'll never be able to forgive your offender.

» Spiritual depth and emotional health will never replace your hurt and bitterness until you make the choice to forgive and heal—and that choice is only yours to make.

PRACTICE #3

Change Your Habits

CHAPTER TEN

The Overstimulated Soul

"The soul that rises from sin to devotion may be compared to the dawning of the day, which at its approach does not expel the darkness instantaneously but only little by little."

- **Francis de Sales**

Researchers at Columbia University wanted to better understand first impressions and snap judgments, specifically in the area of romance. They were curious to see if what people say they want in a partner lines up with the qualities they find attractive in the first few minutes of interaction.

To evaluate this, they created a "speed date" experiment: A dozen men and women filled out a short questionnaire asking them to rate, on a scale of 1 to 10, what they were looking for in a potential partner. The categories were attractiveness, shared interests, sense of humor, sincerity, intelligence, and ambition.

Next, in the back of a bar across the street from the campus, the men rotated seats every few minutes to meet the women sitting across the table for the first time. After each speed date, the participants rated the person they just met on a scale of 1 to 10, based on the same categories. For example, Sarah rated John: attractiveness (7), shared interests (5), sense of humor (8), sincerity (8), intelligence (6), and ambition (7).

Finally, the participants used the 1 to 10 scale to rate the qualities most important to them three more times—immediately after the event, a month later, and six months later.

With this comprehensive collection of exactly what participants were looking for and how they felt immediately after each "date," researchers could compare what a person says they want to what they *actually* want, or at least what they initially find attractive. In other words, they could tell us how good we are at predicting what we will like.

Would it surprise you to know that when they compared what the speed daters said they wanted with what they were actually attracted to, the two answers didn't match? Interestingly, when participants filled out the questionnaire the day after the event, their answers changed. If Sarah is looking for someone intelligent and sincere, but meets and likes men during the experiment who are attractive and funny, then she'll describe her perfect man as attractive and funny. But that effect is short-lasting. A month later, she will again tell you she's looking for an intelligent and sincere partner.

This is a confusing aspect of human nature! Sarah can have clear priorities, but when presented with a room of choices, she changes her mind without even recognizing the change. Sarah is a lot like you and me—we don't like what we want as much as we want what we like.

So what does speed dating have to do with the third practice—*Change Your Habits*? It speaks to a contradiction we all feel in our lives: what we say we want and what we'll settle for are very different things.

Up to this point in the book, we've talked a lot about feelings, because you have to know the truth about the condition of your soul. But we must be careful not to assume that deep change is predominantly felt, because it's not—it's practiced. If the Christian life has any substance to it, it needs to get into your day; that is, into the realm of routine, habitual responses, and casual reactions. Becoming a Christian gives you the power to live a completely different life, but that transformation doesn't just magically happen—it requires action.

At the risk of sounding overly simplistic, there are certain actions Christians perform in order to become more like Jesus. That also means that not performing certain actions makes you less like Jesus. This simple concept is often tragically misunderstood because we confuse the ideas of faith and grace.

A Christian is saved by grace through faith in Jesus Christ, and this is based entirely on what Jesus did, not what you do. You can't take any credit for your salvation, because all you contribute is your sin. This idea is fundamental to deep change because until you believe your salvation is not based on your behavior, you will live under the pressure of performance, and everything you do for God will really be for yourself—to quiet the voices of insecurity and scarcity.

But while faith gives you a relationship with Jesus, it does not make you *like* Jesus—that requires choices. Grace saves you, but it doesn't make decisions for you. In order to experience deep change, you have to change your habits, because while you are saved by faith, you grow and heal through practice. But this is easier said than done.

The Apostle Paul wrote what has to be the most relatable verse in the entire Bible when he said, "I want to do what is good, but I don't. I don't want to do what is wrong, but I do it anyway." Consider for a moment every time you were motivated to make a change for the better in your life. Maybe you wanted to eat healthier, read your Bible, save money, or end a toxic relationship. Did you do it? Maybe you talked yourself out of it, or maybe you started but didn't stick with it. Why?

There are scientific answers for why you don't make the choices you want to make. The overwhelming wisdom says you should make your bad choices harder and your good choices more obvious. In other words, hide the potato chips where you can't find them. But there are also spiritual answers. For a Christian, there is something more at stake than your waistline. Every choice is shaping your soul, and your choices become your character traits.

Once you place your faith in Jesus, you have a new identity. You are a child of God, loved by God, and filled with the same power that resurrected Jesus from the dead. At the same time, though, your past experiences—hurts, habits, and hangups—don't just magically go away. With the help of the Holy Spirit and new habits, you start becoming more like the person God created you to be and less like the person you used to be.

This was perfectly illustrated the night Jesus took his disciples to pray in the Garden of Gethsemane before his arrest. Knowing what events lay ahead for them—confrontation with soldiers, an arrest, and eventual crucifixion—Jesus implored His disciples to pray, because "the spirit is willing but the body is weak." But instead of praying, the disciples slept. Later, when the soldiers arrived and Jesus was arrested, every single disciple ran away and abandoned Him.

The lesson here is that there are actions we can practice that make us more capable of making the right decision and responding the right way in the heat of the moment, and when we don't practice those actions, we are less capable. We can't be certain the outcome would have been different had the disciples prayed instead of slept, but it's safe to assume if they had done what Jesus did in private, they would have been more equipped to respond like Him in public. Jesus prayed and was able to keep His cool and not react defensively, while the disciples didn't, and reacted violently and fearfully.

In the example of Peter's denial that same night, despite his sincere good intentions and declarations, and even being warned by Jesus a few hours earlier, he was not able to withstand the relentless pressure of his automatic tendencies in the moment. What Peter needed that night was not more willpower or resolve, but an inner character that had been developed before it was called upon. Unfortunately, that character is not given to us at the moment of conversion. It is day by day and choice by choice that we become a different *kind* of person—a person who is more like Jesus. So the question is, why don't we gladly and consistently make those choices?

Addicted to Anticipation

In the mid-20th century, American psychologist and Harvard professor B. F. Skinner made an accidental but important discovery in the field of addiction. Skinner was testing the addictive tendencies of the brain by rewarding rats with a treat each time they pressed a lever. On this day, however, he had run out of treats. Since they were time-consuming to make, and he didn't want to stop the experiment, he decided to reward the rats only once per minute instead of with every push. Skinner assumed that limiting the reward would cause the rats to push the lever less frequently, but to his surprise, the occasional reward made them push more, not less. This was the first in a long line of studies that discovered the anticipation of an outcome—specifically a reward—is more stimulating than the outcome itself. In other words, human beings enjoy *wanting* something more than we enjoy *having* something—we are addicted to anticipation.

For years, the common belief among scientists was that dopamine was a reward experienced by addicts fulfilling their addiction, and that's true for the first experience or two, but the part of your brain responsible for seeking pleasure quickly makes a switch, and dopamine releases not when you experience the activity you want, but when you anticipate it.

This makes sense when you think about addiction, but what does it have to do with becoming more like Jesus?

The Apostle Paul, who bemoaned the misery of his struggle to do what he knew he should do, gave an explanation. He said, "there is another power within me that is at war with my mind. This power makes me a slave to the sin that is still within me." As we have already learned, you do not start a relationship with Jesus with a blank canvas. Yes, your sins are forgiven, but your desires, beliefs, and tendencies are "still within you," alongside your new heart. This means that every time you go to make a choice, you are fighting against something incredibly powerful—your history.

You have a way of life that you have tweaked and customized subconsciously to give you the result you want, even if it's not what you say you want. Yes, you say you're too busy, and you want to slow down, but there is an emotional reward that busyness gives you that is not as rewarding as stillness. You want to read your Bible more and scroll on your phone less, but there is a subconscious satisfaction that you experience when you mindlessly scroll that feels more rewarding than scripture. Your relationship with Jesus conflicts with all the other relationships in your life—your relationship with food, technology, money, sex, and anything else that scratches the itch of your discontentment.

We tend to think of the "power" we fight against as the devil, and on some level it is, but it's also the power of habit. The barrier to deep change is both demons *and* dopamine—the emotional rewards you receive from the day-to-day activities in your life that keep you busy, distracted, and discontent.

This helps explain why it's such a struggle to perform the popular Christian practices like Bible reading, prayer, and generosity. We make the mistake of assuming that just because we are Christians and know we *need* to read the Bible, we will also *want* to. We assume it will be easy to gladly give up our old way of life, especially the behaviors that were harmful, but in reality we underestimate just how weak we are, and how much we crave our routines.

When humans rescue baby animals in the wild, the animals are said to be "imprinted," and from that point on the animals will believe that all good things come from people. They can no longer live on their own because they define where they belong by who's taking care of them. Every time you mindlessly grab your phone to stave off boredom, or eat more sugary foods, or add items to your Amazon cart, or overcommit your schedule, you are quieting the discomfort of your interior life, and learning to depend on that subconscious satisfaction for survival.

This is why spiritual disciplines* are crucial for deep change. They are the solution to the ways of life that have "rescued" you from the discomfort of your interior life. Fasting, for instance, is an ancient discipline that combats the emotional rewards of food and the attachment they have to your soul. Silence combats the emotional rewards of distraction. The practices of generosity and frugality combat the emotional rewards of possessing and buying more things we don't need.

We will talk much more in depth about spiritual disciplines in the next chapter, but before we talk about behavior, it's imperative to understand why these disciplines are necessary. You may have never considered daily functions such as eating, leaving your house, or spending money as forces fighting against your spiritual growth, but they very much are. They are the repeated actions that have rewarded

---

* Also known as spiritual habits

your brain for years, and are the habits that your heart, soul, mind, and strength have come to depend on to quiet the discomfort of your private life. We assume this is true for someone with an alcohol or drug addiction, but the truth is we are all addicted in some form or another. We depend on certain activities to make life bearable or enjoyable. Like the creature says in the classic novel, *Frankenstein*, "I was the slave, not the master, of an impulse, which I detested, yet could not disobey … an element which I had willingly chosen." That's the power of a repeated action—eventually, what was once a choice becomes an impulse, and while you could technically decide right now to stop or change, when you try, you learn that you need the emotional rewards those activities—even the unhealthy ones—provide. In a way, you could say that every action is an attempt to fix your feelings.

Even with the best of intentions, or the motivation to change your life, overwhelmingly you fall back into the same pattern of behavior because you don't *want* to do what you know you *need* to do. Good intentions are not enough to become more like Jesus. In order to change deeply and become a different *kind* of person, you have to make different choices and redefine what actions feel rewarding. Until you do, your obedience will always feel like compliance or duty and you will work to muster enough willpower to abstain from doing the things you really want to do. British humorist Sir A.P. Herbert described this perfectly when he jokingly said, "Thank heaven, I have given up smoking again! God! I feel it. Homicidal, but fit. A different man. Irritable, moody, depressed, rude, nervy, perhaps; but the lungs are fine."

That's not the type of life God wants for you—a life of miserable obedience. No, He wants a life of joyful submission. This is why spiritual disciplines are so important, because our hearts are shaped by the actions we perform again and again. In the next chapter you will learn the habits of Jesus and Christians over thousands of years that have helped to redefine what feels rewarding and create new desires. Your habits and choices up to this point in your life have preprogrammed how you respond to stress, insecurity, anger, boredom, and any other feeling. Spiritual disciplines are the way you reprogram those instinctive responses, until eventually you become the *kind* of person who more naturally acts and reacts like Jesus. This means that becoming more like Jesus, and less like the person you've always been, will require new instincts. That only happens through the deep work of the Holy Spirit and the spiritual disciplines you will learn in the next chapter.

Chapter Summary

» Becoming a Christian gives you the power to live a completely different life, but that transformation doesn't just magically happen—it requires action.

» The barrier to deep change is the emotional rewards you receive from the day-to-day activities in your life that keep you busy, distracted, and discontent.

» Your relationship with Jesus conflicts with all the other relationships in your life—your relationship with food, technology, money, sex, and anything else that scratches the itch of your discontentment.

» Spiritual disciplines are the way you reprogram your instinctive responses, until eventually you become the kind of person who more naturally acts and reacts like Jesus.

CHAPTER ELEVEN

Spiritual Disciplines

> "After the first few steps in the Christian life we
> realise that everything which really needs to be
> done in our souls can be done only by God."
> -C. S. Lewis

In the last chapter, you learned how your routine behaviors provide an emotional reward to your brain. This explains why it can feel so challenging to replace old habits with new ones—specifically spiritual habits. But more importantly, it reminds us that every area of our life is a spiritual matter—from the reason we impulsively pick up our phone, to why we overschedule, overcommit, spend too much money, overeat, view pornography, use drugs, or stay in bad relationships. There is no area of your life that is outside the spiritual realm. You are heart, soul, mind, and strength, which means your relationship with Jesus must confront every area of your life. In this chapter, you will learn the habits Christians have practiced for thousands of years to help them become more like Jesus, not just in deed, but in essence.

Let me start by asking you a question: How would you spend your day if you believed you were completely loved by God? Think about it. If from the moment you opened your eyes in the morning until your day was complete, you never for a second doubted that God loved you and was pleased with you, that you had nothing to prove and nothing to earn, and you couldn't mess that up, how would you spend your day?

Of course you would still have responsibilities to fulfill, like work and family, but how would that day be different than any other day if you truly believed God was "well pleased" with you?

This is a challenging question to answer because we rarely recognize all the ways our unsettledness drives our actions. For example, we rarely admit the reason we can't sit in silence is because it scares us; instead we say, I don't have the time, or I'm busy. It's true we're busy, but we make time for the things that satisfy us subconsciously, and we avoid the things that don't.

Truly believing you are fully loved by God would remove all insecurity and uneasiness. This means that you would be comfortable being alone and quiet. You would enjoy nice things but not have to have them. You would feel sexual desires but not feel entitled to them. You would be okay with not receiving attention or applause, and you would gladly give of yourself for the sake of someone else. In a variety of different expressions, you wouldn't need any outside factors to convince you of your worth.

The life I just described is the life Jesus lived—a life without any insecurity. The degree to which we struggle with these issues, like being uncomfortable with stillness, or desiring luxuries and attention, reveals how badly we need to become more convinced of our worth and believe we are completely loved and accepted by God. This is why we need to practice counter-instinctual habits—*spiritual disciplines*.

A spiritual discipline is any activity that makes you more capable of receiving more of God's life and power.* God doesn't need you to read your Bible, pray, give, or anything else. These habits don't alter the way God sees you or feels about you, but they do alter the way you see and feel about yourself. Spiritual disciplines are the way Christians are formed and shaped, and experience God's presence and power. They enable you to live more like Jesus lived for the right reasons—with nothing to earn, only everything to receive.

While technically a spiritual discipline could be any activity, historians agree that there are at least 15 habits that are consistent in the life of Jesus and the history of the church. They are split into two categories: *disciplines of abstinence* and *disciplines of engagement*. (See image 11.1)

Looking at a list of this length can feel daunting. How can someone do all of these things, and do them well? But remember, becoming like Jesus cannot be earned, only learned. There is no pressure to become really good at spiritual disciplines; there is instead an invitation to practice Jesus' way of life. I love the way C. S. Lewis describes this difference in *Mere Christianity*: "It is more like painting a portrait than like obeying a set of rules. And the odd

---

* It's important to note that this is any activity that does not include harming yourself or others. Unfortunately, there are some who use religious practices to inflict personal harm, believing that this helps them more relate to the experience of Christ, but this is not what is modeled and taught by Jesus or the Apostles.

Disciplines of Abstinence	Disciplines of Engagement
Solitude	Study
Silence	Worship
Fasting	Celebration
Frugality	Service
Chastity	Prayer
Secrecy	Fellowship
Sacrifice	Confession
	Submission

Image 11.1

thing is that while in one way it is much harder than keeping rules, in another way it is far easier. The real Son of God is at your side. He is beginning to turn you into the same kind of thing as Himself. He is beginning, so to speak, to 'inject' His kind of life and thought, His Zoe, into you…"

Another thing to notice about the list of disciplines is how varied it is in style, personality, and practice. This cannot be overstated. In many churches, prayer and Bible study are held up as *the* activities that will give you a deeply satisfying relationship with God, but very few people actually succeed in using prayer and Bible study to attain the spiritual richness they desire, and instead, many find them to be inconvenient or lifeless. The truth is, statistically speaking, a small percentage of those talking about these practices are actually doing what they promote.

The tools you have at your disposal to experience God in a deeply personal way are much greater than just prayer and Bible reading.

In order to experience deep change, it's important to begin to see how your days and weeks are filled with countless opportunities to engage with God. Even in "ordinary" events, like serving someone, saving money, or spending time with friends, you can experience more of the life and power of Jesus.

Let me give you a brief summary of each habit. First, let's examine the disciplines of abstinence.[**]

Disciplines of Abstinence

In the disciplines of abstinence, you abstain to a certain degree and for a certain time from the satisfaction of "normal and legitimate" desires, in order to recognize and retrain your instinctual behavioral tendencies. It's important to remember that you do not abstain from these activities because they are inherently bad, but instead to tame legitimate desires gone wrong.

Cambridge professor and Anglican priest William Ralph Inge beautifully described this balance when he said, "If we feel that any habit or pursuit, harmless in itself, is keeping us from God and sinking us deeper in the things of earth; if we find that things which others can do with impunity are for us the occasion of falling, then abstinence is our only course. Abstinence alone can recover for us the real value of what should have been for our help but which has been an occasion of falling… it is necessary that we should steadily resolve to give up anything that comes between ourselves and God." That is what you're doing when you make the choice to practice

---

[**] Many of the concepts and definitions shared here can be found in Chapter 9 of Dallas Willard's book *The Spirit of the Disciplines*.

disciplines of abstinence. Let's examine each one:

Solitude is the practice of abstaining from interaction. In solitude, you purposefully deny yourself companionship and all that comes from interacting with others. The purpose is to find freedom from the ingrained behaviors and routines that you perform when you are around people—the kind of role-playing Jesus warned his disciples about. Thomas à Kempis reminded us of our great need for solitude when he said, "as often times as I was among men I came back a less man, that is to say less holy."

Silence is the practice of abstaining from noise. In silence, you close off your soul from sounds—noise, music, or words—in order to sense and concentrate on the presence of God. Silence is incredibly rare these days, but when we do have the opportunity to experience it, we often drown it out with music or background noise. In general, humans are very uncomfortable with silence. A study at the University of Virginia showed that, given the choice, many preferred undergoing electric shock to sitting alone with their thoughts.[***] Nothing reveals the anxiety of your interior life like silence, but as Eberhard Arnold observes, "people who love one another can be silent together."

Fasting is the practice of abstaining from food, and possibly drink, for some significant, predetermined period of time. In a way, it is choosing to be hungry so you can feel more of a hunger for

---

[***] Study participants were exposed to a mild shock, which they all reported they didn't like and would pay money not to undergo again. But when left alone in an empty room with a "shocker" button for up to 15 minutes, removed from all distractions, unable to check their phone or listen to music, two-thirds of men and one-fourth of women in the study chose to voluntarily shock themselves rather than sit in silence.

SPIRITUAL DISCIPLINES

God. Like silence, fasting quickly teaches you a lot about yourself, like how much you depend on the pleasures of eating to hide the discomfort of your life. As you begin to practice fasting, there will almost certainly be a feeling of embarrassment when you learn just how strong your cravings for food are, but as you continue in it, you become more able to deny yourself and experience a sustaining presence from God. Jesus told the disciples that it is possible to fast and not appear to others as if you feel miserable. It will take time, but eventually you will experience a joy in fasting that far supersedes the pleasures of food.

Frugality is the practice of abstaining from using money or goods. In frugality, you are choosing to purchase only items that are necessary, and avoid items that merely gratify. There are many spiritual benefits to this practice, but there are also practical benefits, like avoiding debt. John Joseph Surin was once asked why, "when so many people seem to wish to be great in God's eyes, there are so few who are truly saintly. 'The chief reason,' he replied, 'is that they give too big a place in life to indifferent things.'" Frugality helps free you from a life preoccupied by indifferent things, and focus on "what is better."

Chastity is the practice of abstaining from sex—choosing not to engage in sexual relations in order to free yourself from feelings of entitlement to sexual desires. Similarly to how fasting causes you to realize how much you crave food, chastity makes you aware of just how strongly your sexual desires influence your life. But Jesus taught his disciples that it is possible to willingly sacrifice sexual pleasure for the Kingdom of God. Chastity helps us learn that just because we feel a desire does not mean we are entitled to fulfill it. This is one of the more foreign concepts in our culture, and through the wrong lens or taught with the wrong motives it could be seen as a type of sexual repression, but as Dietrich Bonhoeffer said, "the essence of chastity is not the suppression of lust but the total orientation of one's life toward a goal."

Secrecy is the practice of abstaining from drawing attention to yourself. In choosing secrecy, you are concealing your good qualities and accomplishments in order to help you tame the hunger for acclaim, justification, or attention. In time, we "learn to love to be unknown and even to accept misunderstanding without the loss of our peace, joy, or purpose," and experience a relationship with God free from the opinions of others. The Gospel accounts show us how hard Jesus tried to avoid large crowds and recognition for His acts because He trusted that God would determine when He needed to be known and noticed. While typically not thought of as a spiritual habit, secrecy can be a great source of joy, as you come to long for others around you to be more noticed, celebrated, and recognized than yourself—to genuinely rejoice at their success.

Sacrifice is the practice of abstaining from meeting your needs with your resources. Where frugality has you abstain from anything unnecessary, sacrifice goes further, in choosing to abstain from what is essential for life. In sacrifice, you forfeit the security of meeting your needs in total abandonment to God, trusting that He will provide. We see examples of this in the Bible when Abraham took his son Isaac to Mt. Moriah, and the widow gave her last two coins in the offering. It's important to clarify that this is not the same thing as carelessness—it is an intentional act to not provide a solution, trusting that God can and will. As Dallas Willard warns, "the cautious faith that never saws off the limb on which it is sitting never learns that unattached limbs may find strange, unaccountable ways of not falling."

We will examine the disciplines of engagement in a moment, but first, stop and think about each spiritual habit you just read about. What would it feel like to be comfortable in isolation and quiet, to not be at the mercy of the pleasures of food, sex, or luxuries, and to be free from the pressure to defend yourself, draw attention to yourself, or provide for yourself? Imagine that life for a moment. This is the life Jesus lived, and while not perfectly attainable, it is available to you too.

Disciplines of Engagement

The disciplines of engagement are the perfect complement to the disciplines of abstinence. Where habits like silence, fasting, and frugality help you retrain your body away from sins of indulgence, the disciplines of engagement help you fight the human tendency to disengage from the activities your soul needs to flourish. Similarly to the time Jesus healed the lame man and commanded him to "take up [his] mat and walk," the disciplines of engagement implore you to take action—to live out your faith in the real world among others. Let's examine each one:

Study is the practice of engaging with the written and spoken word of God. It cannot be overstated how important the practice of study is in the life of a Christian, because it's how we come to learn what is true about God. Jesus said that someone who builds their life on His words is like living in a house with a solid foundation, but someone who doesn't is like living in a house that crumbles every time a storm comes. Reading the Bible, meditating on it, and memorizing it separates actual lived faith from superstition. As Calvin Miller said, "Mystics without study are only spiritual romantics who want relationship without effort." Our prayer is always that God would speak to us through His word and teach us objective truths that can be lived out in real life.

Worship is the practice of expressing your love for God through thoughts, words, rituals, and symbols. We should do this both when we're alone and when we're gathered together with other believers. Depending on your religious background, you may have different ideas or imagery for what worship should look like. Unfortunately, worship has become categorized by style, but it is more than a worship service or songs that you sing. Worship is any effort put forth to express the greatness, beauty, or goodness of God. This is another reason why study is so important—it teaches you about God and gives you more reasons to worship him.

Celebration is the practice of enjoying yourself based on your faith and confidence in God. In a way, celebration is the final step in worship. Where worship is primarily about who God is, celebration is about giving thanks for what God has done for you. Many Christians wouldn't think of celebration as a spiritual discipline, but the Old Testament is filled with instructions for God's people to take extended breaks from their work for festivals and celebrations, specifically to remember what God had done for His people and express their gratitude. "We dishonor God as much by fearing and avoiding pleasure as we do by depending on it or living for it." A Christian who does not celebrate may not yet fully grasp what they have received in Jesus Christ.

Service is the practice of using your resources and strength for the good of others. Non-Christians can serve people as well, but what makes service a spiritual discipline is *intent*. There's certainly nothing wrong with doing a good thing simply because it's a good thing to do, but for a Christian, service can be a means to combat arrogance, possessiveness, selfishness, or any other negative emotion that is keeping you from experiencing more of the life and power of Jesus. Service out of obligation only creates resentment and bitterness, but ironically, service as a spiritual habit frees you from feeling obligated to do it. It gives you the freedom and humility to accept that you are no better or worse than your peers and are not above serving anyone who might be in need.

Prayer is the practice of communicating with God through words or thoughts. As with other disciplines, and to an even greater degree, it's a habit that is strengthened and becomes more natural with practice. Praying regularly gives you the confidence and instincts to pray more—moment by moment—throughout the events of your day. As we have already learned from Jesus' warning to the disciples in the garden, prayer is a way to strengthen our spiritual resolve and lessen the power of our sinful instincts. There is no "one size fits all" format to prayer, but Jesus instructed his disciples to try to be alone in a quiet place, and let go of the pressure to use a lot of words— that's a great place to start.

Fellowship is the practice of engaging in spiritual disciplines with other Christians. While we each have a personal relationship with God, Christianity was never intended to be practiced only in isolation. We need each other for the sake of our souls. When believers gather together to pray, worship, study, give, or serve, there is the potential for power that is different when practiced alone. Fellowship also encourages us to learn how to love and appreciate the differences within our community of faith. The Bible teaches us that each and every person has God-given qualities that are needed by the church from time to time. Through fellowship, we learn to love those we might naturally avoid.

Confession is the practice of telling others you trust about your most vulnerable weaknesses and failures. It's an extension of fellowship, in that as we learn to love and trust one another, we take the agonizing step to drop our pretense and admit our humanity. Confession removes the psychological and physical burden that comes from hidden sin. As we practice confession, we learn to be loved based on not only our strengths, but also our weaknesses.

Submission is the practice of choosing to follow someone's leadership. In submission, you reject the power structure of the culture that promotes "onward and upward" mobility, and instead model yourself after the attitude of Jesus, who, "though He was God, did not think of equality with God as something to cling to. Instead, He gave up His divine privileges; and took the humble position of a servant." It's important to note that submission cannot be forced; in order to be a spiritual discipline, it must be a willing choice. It requires humility to believe that someone else might have wisdom you are lacking, or might see something about you that you cannot see in yourself.

Before moving on, stop and think about the spiritual habits of engagement you've just read. Imagine for a moment feeling like you are growing in knowledge and intimacy with God, and you belong to a community of faith that refuses to let you hide—a group of Christians who you want to be with and serve because they bring you genuine joy and you trust them enough to be vulnerable and follow their leadership, even if it requires sacrifice.

$3 Worth of God

One of the central goals of this book is not just changing what we do, but changing what we want to do—becoming a different *kind* of person who desires different activities. The spiritual disciplines we've discussed in this chapter can feel incredibly rewarding, but when you consider some of the habits, like solitude, silence, chastity, and submission, it's easy to understand why many people struggle to imagine getting any sense of satisfaction from them. That's because up to this point in life, you've taught yourself to instinctively seek satisfaction from other activities.

It's possible you have tried to practice some of these before, and your experience was uninspiring. Maybe you think "I tried and I wasn't good at it." Exactly! No one is naturally gifted or inclined toward spiritual activities. I'm not trying to mislead you into believing that you will jump out of bed wanting to confess your sins and abstain from food. Of course you won't! But the more you practice, the more you retrain your heart, soul, mind, and strength to crave these spiritual habits instead of the dependencies you previously developed. There will definitely be a season when you have to make yourself do them even though you're not naturally inclined to.

While writing this book, I've been practicing 10 minutes of silence each morning. I start a timer and sit in my chair in the quiet. Most days feel spiritually beneficial, but ironically, this morning before writing about the importance of silence, I was extremely distracted and unsettled. I was surrounded by moving boxes and unfolded laundry, and my mind kept drifting off in so many different directions. At one point, I stopped the timer, started it over, and whispered to God, "Sorry about that, let's try again." But the second time wasn't any better—in fact, it was probably worse.

It's funny how our sinful nature tries to convince us that it's not enough to practice spiritual disciplines, but that we also have to be highly proficient at them. Shame shows up and tries to convince you that since you are struggling to focus or you didn't "get anything out of it," you must be doing it wrong or you're not as spiritual as you claim to be. But the truth is, my time in silence this morning did exactly what it was supposed to do. It revealed the things that are preoccupying my mind and heart and revealed the areas of my life that are making my soul feel unsettled. Distractions only reveal that we are human and that we desperately need the very thing we are attempting to do.

This is where the great mystery of grace begins to reveal itself. In one sense, the change you desperately desire requires your active participation, but in another sense, the qualities you seek—love, joy, peace, patience, kindness, goodness, faithfulness, gentleness, and self-control—cannot be manufactured, only grown. Virtue cannot be forced. Goodness and gentleness cannot be squeezed out. No amount of pressure can stimulate your faith in Christ. Like the boy with only a few fish and loaves, we bring our meager attempts and resources to God, and He supernaturally multiplies them to produce far more than they should be able to produce on their own. Our task, then, is simply to cooperate with God—to show up, try, and offer ourselves the best we can—and in time, disproportionate to our proficiencies, we begin to transform, taking on the personality of Christ, and behaving as He would behave.

The painful question you must answer is, do you want that? I don't mean, "would it be nice if that happened?" I mean, do you want to find a satisfying and deeply rewarding life in exactly the opposite way as your friends and neighbors will attempt to obtain it? As you consider the prospect of a moment-by-moment relationship with the Holy Spirit, there are legitimate concerns about the practicality of it. The idea that Christian faith should be the framework for *all* of life's choices and events feels a bit extreme, doesn't it? Don't some sacrifices have to be made for the sake of pragmatism? In some ways, we do believe serious Christian commitment can lead to a meaningful life, but it's not the *only* way, right? We're still not completely convinced that there isn't an amount of money, love, status, influence, or control that could also satisfy the dissatisfaction we feel. We're not opposed to wholehearted commitment to Jesus—for those who want to choose that route—but it's costly.

It reminds me of a stinging poem written by Wilbur Rees,

"I would like to buy $3 worth of God, please.
Not enough to explode my soul or disturb my sleep,
but just enough to equal a cup of warm milk
or a snooze in the sunshine.
I don't want enough of God
to make me love a black man
or pick beets with a migrant.
I want ecstasy, not transformation.
I want the warmth of a womb, not a new birth.
I want a pound of the Eternal in a paper sack.
I'd like to buy $3 worth of God, please."

So again, we come face to face with the reality of what is holding us back from the deep change we want. It's less vile evils and more the subconscious satisfaction of being entertained, problem solving, success, food, spending money, and being in control. The life and power of Jesus available to you is just on the other side of the life you've come to love.

Let's end this chapter by examining what current instinctual responses are preventing you from experiencing more of the life and power of Jesus. Where are you distracting yourself, or silencing discomfort? I've provided a list of potential answers below, but there are many more options than I've listed.

- Eating (from boredom or addiction)
- Over-scheduling
- Problem solving / trying to control situations

SPIRITUAL DISCIPLINES

- Media consumption
- Spending money / buying needless things
- Smartphone usage

As you consider this list, fight the urge to wallow in guilt and shame. Yes, you are not as much like Jesus as you want to be, but you have awareness and the tools to help you begin to experience His life and power to a greater degree than ever before. As you consider what's hindering you, also think about which spiritual disciplines you feel are most important to implement in your life to counteract your tendencies. Take a moment and pray the words of Psalm 19 as you begin.

> *How can I know all the sins lurking in my heart?*
> *Cleanse me from these hidden faults.*
> *Keep your servant from deliberate sins!*
> *Don't let them control me.*
> *Then I will be free of guilt*
> *and innocent of great sin.*
> *May the words of my mouth*
> *and the meditation of my heart*
> *be pleasing to you,*
> *O Lord, my rock and my redeemer.*
> *Amen.*

Chapter Summary

» A spiritual discipline is any activity that makes you more capable of receiving more of God's life and power.

» In the disciplines of abstinence, you abstain to a certain degree and for a certain time from the satisfaction of "normal and legitimate" desires, in order to recognize and retrain your instinctual behavioral tendencies.

» The disciplines of abstinence are solitude, silence, fasting, frugality, chastity, secrecy, and sacrifice.

» The disciplines of engagement implore you to take action—to live out your faith in the real world among others.

» The disciplines of engagement are study, worship, celebration, service, prayer, fellowship, confession, and submission.

» What is holding us back from deep change is less vile evils and more the subconscious satisfaction of being entertained, problem solving, success, food, spending money, and being in control.

CHAPTER TWELVE

Something More Beautiful

> "I can resist everything except temptation."
> -Oscar Wilde

As we have learned, it is day by day and choice by choice that we become a different *kind* of person—a person who is more like Jesus. And while many of our subconscious choices provide us with emotional rewards, we also make very deliberate choices to engage in sinful activity. These are more than our "normal" daily rituals; they are our secret sins—our private struggles—and they are the worst, most embarrassing parts of us. As you begin to practice spiritual disciplines, you will be forced to confront your most humiliating habits, because deep change cannot occur as long as you try to compartmentalize your character. You must address the deeply ingrained and long-standing deliberate sins that seem impossible to overcome. In this chapter we will look specifically at the importance of resisting temptation.

Temptation is nothing new, but the speed and degree to which you can do harm to yourself or others in an attempt to escape, cope, or avoid is more dangerous now than ever. You can do enough damage in a 10-minute online shopping spree to wreck your life for years. As a pastor, I talk to people all the time who feel hopeless and powerless against their vices. Some are fighting the extremes of life-threatening addictions, and others simply would like to eliminate the bad habits that are holding them back. What all of these conversations have in common is a feeling of helplessness, as if defeat is inevitable. There seems to be an assumption that no one is capable of living a truly victorious life free from sin—that we are all guaranteed a certain percentage of "slipups" throughout our day. While it's of course true that no one is completely sinless, this doesn't mean we have to be dominated by sin, or stuck in cycles of bondage and defeat. It is possible to be stronger than your urges.

As you begin to practice spiritual disciplines to counteract your instinctual tendencies, you need to be prepared to face more adversity than you anticipate. I wish I could tell you the devil will stay out of your way, but he doesn't fight fair, and you will find an onslaught of temptation on the other side of your decision to change. At the very moment when you make the decision to experience more of the power and life of Jesus, you will be able to think of 10,000 reasons not to. Your vices will scream louder, embarrassment will cause you to turn inward and hide your struggles, and fear of a future without your dependencies will cause you to wonder if you're not better off with the life you have. It's at that moment when you must resist the urge to return to your old ways, because nothing will drain you of the power and life of Jesus faster than deliberate sin.

Much of the discourse about sin and temptation isn't as helpful as we would hope, because it's primarily talked about in terms of techniques and "hacks" to prevent us from giving in. While there are certainly times when the furnace of temptation burns so hot we need strategies to prevent our fall, in general, this is a shortsighted view of sin and the need for restraint. It's based on the assumption that we are powerless against our desires, and blames outside factors for our failures. Tragically, this has done great harm to Christians, especially in the area of purity. We have talked about sexual desires as if they are uncontrollable and we are entitled to fulfill them, and we have used a message of modesty to shame women and give men an excuse to lack self-control. We keep looking for methods to escape our impulses because we assume it's the best we can do. But there's a better way.

In Greek mythology there was an island known as the "land of the sirens" inhabited by three creatures, each with the body of a bird and the face of a woman, who could sing so beautifully they were able to lure sailors to the island and shipwreck them.

The most famous story of the sirens is probably from the Odyssey. On a quest to return home, Odysseus knew the danger ahead, so he put wax in the ears of his men to keep them from hearing the songs and changing course. But Odysseus, wanting to hear the sirens sing, had his sailors tie him to the mast, and instructed them that under no circumstances were they to untie his ropes until they passed the island. When Odysseus heard the sirens, he strained to get free, but was unable to. So Odysseus and his men eluded destruction and continued on their journey.

While successful, Odysseus' passage past the sirens' island is quite different from that of another story of Jason and the Argonauts. They too avoided death on the rocks of the sirens. However, instead of binding themselves or using wax, Jason had a lute player named Orpheus travel with him. Orpheus was highly skilled and able to captivate his audience as long as he played. As soon as Jason's ship came near the island of the sirens, the crew assembled on deck in the shadow of the mast and Orpheus began playing his enchanting melodies. The men were able to pass safely and continued on their journey because they were captivated by something more beautiful.

The stories of Odysseus and Jason help us understand two distinct strategies for trying to resist temptation. One strategy is to avoid shipwreck through sheer force. Using this strategy, we don't attempt to change our desires, we simply create techniques to try to avoid giving in to them. But there is another, more effective strategy—what Ted Moon calls "the sweetness of sanctified living." This way focuses on something more beautiful and more satisfying than cheap gratification. You focus less on trying to avoid sin in the moment, and instead adopt a way of life that avoids the feelings that lead to temptation to begin with. Sadly, many Christians either feel like a prisoner to passion, or feel as if they are chained to the Christian life against their will. Many live under the pressure and guilt of trying not to disappoint God. This inevitably leads to a crushing demand for avoidance and willpower.

We often think of willpower as an extraordinary force to be summoned to deal with emergencies, but you can't continuously succeed if you try to face temptation head-on and resist in the moment of choice. In order to find freedom from the sins that keep you stuck, you need something more than temptation techniques—you need Christian character.

Sinner and Saint

Character speaks to the *kind* of person you are—the things you want to do and are willing to do. This can only be revealed in time, through reviewing the patterns of your behavior that happen more or less automatically. So when I say Christian character, I am describing the kind of life you can and should live instinctually—a life of freedom, purity, and integrity—not because you learn how to fake it, but because that is the kind of person you are. As Christians, we typically downplay our dysfunction and justify our behavior by saying that it was just a slipup—it's not who we really are. But we give ourselves too much credit, and in denying the truth about our condition, we keep ourselves from finding the freedom we desperately want. We must be honest about who we are, and more importantly, how sinful we are.

The painful truth is that someone who lies is the *kind* of person who would lie. We can argue that they have a good reason for lying, or that their lies don't do harm, but we can't say they are not the kind of person who would lie. The same is true for other sinful behaviors too—stealing, cheating, sex, gossip, etc. As uncomfortable as it is, we have to confront our worst, most humiliating qualities and admit that we are the *kind* of people who would do something like that. As long as we blame outside forces for our habitual sins, we deny ourselves the greatest tool we have in our journey for freedom:

personal choice. We are responsible for our character, and where there is anything in our life we wish we could stop doing, we have to first admit that these actions are not slipups, but rather an accurate portrayal of the *kind* of person we are.

How does that make you feel? Admitting to yourself that you are not as ethical, principled, or disciplined as you claim to be is disheartening, but it is necessary for repentance. You are combating self-deception and coming to terms with how badly you need grace. Think of it as a "saint" and "sinner" version of yourself—two coexisting identities that wage war for your soul. (See image 12.1)

We do ourselves a grave disservice when we imply that we don't struggle or sin. Yes, our sins have been forgiven, but our sinful nature still exists, and while the sin that lives in you can be minimized, it will never completely go away. You are strong and weak, loving and hateful, humble and arrogant, all at the same time. It can be deflating

Saint	Sinner
Vulnerable	Defensive
Strong	Weak
Secure	Insecure
Kind	Hurtful
Peaceful	Violent
Loving	Hateful
Humble	Arrogant
Truthful	Dishonest
Trustworthy	Hypocritical
Capable	Helpless/Victim

Image 12.1

to come face to face with your worst characteristics, which is why so many Christians live in denial, but your worst qualities should not surprise you. You must come to terms with the extensive damage sin has done to every part of who you are—heart, soul, mind, and strength.

Now for some good news—you do not have to resign yourself to a life of defeat. The power of sin is strong, but you *can* help it. Your sin is great, but Jesus is greater. The urges and temptations that pull you away are powerful, but you are *not* powerless. You are filled with the power of Jesus and able to develop Christian character leading to a life of freedom!

Knowing the effect your interior life has on your actions, it's obvious that the answer to temptation doesn't lie in simply trying to trick your behavior—it lies somewhere deeper. If you want to find freedom, you must identify the reasons you find your humiliating habits so appealing. Then and only then will you be able to have the upper hand against your most tempting desires.

Image + Idea

At its core, every temptation involves two things: an *image* and an *idea*. The image is the scenario you role-play in your mind for the action you are tempted to perform. Whether you realize it or not, every sin is imagined before it is committed. Second is the idea of what that action will do for you—"If I _____, then I will _____." The ideas and outcomes of sin are much more subtle than "if/then." Most of the time you don't even realize there's an idea attached to your action—you simply want some kind of emotional reward. But almost always, the idea attached to your temptation attempts to resolve the uneasiness in your life.

While this is a very technical way of thinking about temptation, it is important, because temptations are often thought of as random urges, when in fact they are ideas we believe in. Attached to the image of sex, violence, substances, or any other sinful action is an idea, and the degree to which you believe that idea determines your ability to resist. This explains why someone can be stuck repeating the same sins for decades—not simply because the moment of action is gratifying, but because deep down, they believe their feelings *must* be satisfied. They are convinced that whatever their sinful action gives them is what they must have in order to attain a deeply satisfying life—something they cannot find in God. If asked, we would swear we do want to stop. We pray and ask God to help us, but the painful truth is that in our interior life, we are not yet convinced that God can offer us something better than the things we cannot give up.

Think about it for a moment. Do you really believe that a relationship with Jesus can satisfy you more than sex? Do you honestly believe that the joy of the Lord can supply you with something you cannot find in substances? Unfortunately, Christianity has the reputation of being repressive and forcing people to ignore their natural desires. This message is believed because some well-meaning Christians have encouraged people to use a kind of "fake it till you make it" strategy to withstand their urges. But that is a misunderstanding of the Christian faith. We should never try to repress our feelings and desires. Instead, we should be very aware of and honest about their appeal and strength, but not assume we are entitled to fulfill them. We should admit how strongly we feel the pull of sin and ask for prayer and help to *suppress* our desires—fully aware of their influence, but willingly choosing to abstain.

Society defines freedom as being able to do whatever you want whenever you want, with no boundaries or limitations, as long as it doesn't hurt anyone. It promotes this message ad nauseam every minute of the day. But Christianity defines freedom as the ability to *not* do what you want to do. There's a big difference. You are only truly free when you can withstand your urges. What most people define as freedom is actually still bondage, just to something other than religion. If they attempted to stop doing what they wanted to do, they would find it harder than they think.

There's no secret formula for freedom, but there is a practice you learned about in the last chapter that Christians have used for thousands of years to break free from the bondage of sin—the practice of *confession*.

Traditionally, confession is thought of as admitting your mistakes, and it is, but you should also confess the ideas you're believing, the scenarios you're imagining, and the desires you're feeling. The more comfortable you become with admitting your insecurities and desires, the less power they have in your life. Being honest doesn't magically make your desires go away, but there is something supernatural that happens when you let another person know the truth about your condition. Sin begins to lose its power when it becomes public knowledge. In confession, we admit our most embarrassing self, and in return are reminded that we are loved, not because of performance, but because of the work of Christ.

Writing during World War II, C. S. Lewis compared withstanding temptation to establishing army camps further into enemy territory. He said, "Good and evil both increase at compound interest. That is why the little decisions you and I make every day are of such infinite importance. The smallest good act today is the capture of a strategic point from which, a few months later, you may be able to go on to victories you never dreamed of. An apparently trivial indulgence in lust or anger today is the loss of a ridge or railway line or bridgehead from which the enemy may launch an attack otherwise impossible."

Study after study has found that people with more supposed willpower are really just people who rarely need to use it because they do not position themselves in situations requiring hard choices. In other words, character compounds until right decisions are easier to make than wrong ones. With each confession and temptation resisted, you are becoming a different kind of person. You are building a Christian character—a person who is more like Jesus.

What if you decided to confess your actions, ideas, and desires to a trusted friend? It may be the first time you've ever told the truth out loud, but once the secrets that are hiding in the dark are brought into the light, I think you will find they are much less powerful than you think. Before reading any further, commit to confessing to a specific friend on a specific day using this sentence:

I plan on talking to _____ on _____ to confess and share the desires, thoughts, and feelings I'm experiencing, so I can live free from secret sin.

As we end this chapter, ask God to help you find freedom from your most humiliating habits.

Jesus, here I am again,
  desiring things that cause death for my soul.

Given the choice of this moment or eternity,
  let me choose what is eternal.
Given the choice of this easy pleasure, or the harder road of the cross,
  give me grace to follow You.

O Lord, in the furnace of temptation,
  do not let me be deceived,
  believing I might find the peace and satisfaction I long for,
  apart from Your presence.

Faced with temptation,
I would rather choose You, Jesus.
But I am weak,
  so be my strength.
I am shattered,
  so be my life.
I am selfish,
  so remake me now.
Create in me new desires according to the better designs of Your love.

Amen

Chapter Summary

» It is possible to be stronger than your urges.

» Character speaks to the kind of person you are—the things you want to do and are willing to do. This can only be revealed in time, through reviewing the patterns of your behavior that happen more or less automatically.

» Temptation is often thought of as random urges, when in fact they are ideas we believe in. Attached to the image of sex, violence, substances, or any other sinful action is an idea, and the degree to which you believe that idea determines your ability to resist.

» Society defines freedom as being able to do whatever you want whenever you want, with no boundaries or limitations, as long as it doesn't hurt anyone. Christianity defines freedom as the ability to not do what you want to do. You are only truly free when you can withstand your urges.

» The more comfortable you become admitting your insecurities and desires, the less power they have in your life.

PRACTICE #4

Embrace Your Limits

CHAPTER THIRTEEN

The Courage to Say No

"In proportion as our inward life fails, we go more constantly and desperately to the post-office. You may depend on it, that the poor fellow who walks away with the greatest number of letters, proud of his extensive correspondence, has not heard from himself this long while." - **Henry David Thoreau**

In the 1950s, psychologist Solomon Asch wanted to examine the power of peer pressure. To begin each experiment, he would bring a subject into the room with a group of strangers. The subject was unaware that the other participants in the room were actors planted by the researcher and instructed to deliver scripted answers to specific questions.

The group was shown one card with a line on it, and then a second card with a series of lines. Each person was asked to select the line on the second card that was similar in length to the line on the first card. It was a very simple task. (See image 13.1)

The experiment would always begin the same. First, there would

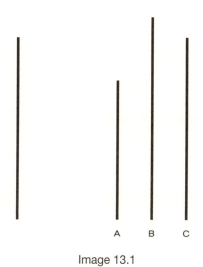

Image 13.1

be some easy trials where everyone agreed on the correct line. Then after a few rounds, the participants were shown a test that was just as obvious as the previous ones, except the actors in the room would intentionally select an incorrect answer. For example, they might respond "A" to the comparison shown above. Everyone planted in the room would agree that the lines were the same length, even though they were clearly different.

The subject, who was unaware of the ruse, would immediately become confused. Their eyes would open wide. They would laugh nervously to themselves, double-checking the reactions of the other participants, growing more agitated as one person after another answered incorrectly. Soon the subject began to doubt their own eyes, and in many cases, they gave the same answer as the actors, even though they knew it was incorrect.

Asch ran this experiment many times and in many different ways. What he discovered was that as the number of actors increased, so did the conformity of the subject. If it was just the subject and one actor, then there was no effect on the person's choice. They just assumed the other person was wrong. When two actors were in the room with the subject, there was still little impact. But as the number of people increased to three actors, then four, then all the way to eight, the subject became more and more likely to second-guess themselves. By the end of the experiment, nearly 75% of the subjects had agreed with the group answer even though it was obviously incorrect.

Asch's research revealed a telling truth about human nature: *whenever we are unsure how to act, we look to the majority to guide our behavior.*

When we read about Asch's peer pressure study, our defense mechanism kicks in and we assure ourselves that given the chance, we would not be one of the weak ones, so easily swayed from the truth. But we give ourselves too much credit. According to the Rogers adoption curve used in business and technology, only 2.5% of people are innovators, and only 13.5% are early adopters. That means 84% of us only do things, or like things, after we believe it's what we're supposed to do. 8 out of 10 of us look to the crowd to define our preferences and beliefs. An honest evaluation of our life would probably reveal that many of our choices—about money, technology, fashion, relationships, or careers—are made simply because everyone else is making them. After all, "everyone can't be wrong, right?"

We've reached the last practice of deep change—*Embrace Your Limits*—and of all the practices, this is by far the most counter-cultural. In a world of constant doing, going, and scrolling, we have become so accustomed to living beyond our limits that the thought of embracing self-imposed boundaries seems illogical. We live in a culture that is constantly bombarding us with the message that we are unlimited—that we can have it all and do it all, and our only limitations are the ones we place on ourselves. We buy it hook, line, and sinker, maxing out our schedules, credit cards, and waistlines, leaving us stressed, anxious, and discontented. As you strive to *feel your feelings*, *face your past*, and *change your habits*, you'll need to embrace a new way of life—one that's less rushed, and more intentional.

You are limited. Whether you accept that or not, it's true. You only have a certain amount of time in a day, and a certain amount of energy, money, and capacity. And while we know this to be factually true, we do not live as if it's practically true. We still commit as if we have more than 24 hours, spend as if we have unlimited money, and give of ourselves as if we have infinite energy. But instead of feeling more productive, affluent, and connected, we are more anxious than ever before. We are in a hurry and in debt—an emotionally bankrupt society that lives on the brink of burnout and outrage. Statistics show that 18% of Americans use a mood-altering substance nearly every day, and 40 million people a year experience an impairment because of an anxiety disorder—and that was before a global pandemic. One study found that 39% of Americans reported being more anxious than they were a year ago.

Our problem isn't that we have anything against depth; it's that we're simply stretched too thin to love God with all our heart, soul, mind, and strength. We are like the people Jesus described in the parable of the great feast, who are invited to the banquet but cannot come because they have too many other seemingly noble obligations. That's what makes embracing limits so challenging. It's rarely the difference between obvious good and evil that causes us to miss real intimacy with God, it's just that we are too preoccupied. We are more busy than bad, more distracted than non-spiritual—more involved in the breaking news of the day than in character development and spiritual depth.

John Piper gave a stinging rebuke when he said, "The greatest enemy of hunger for God is not poison but apple pie. It is not the banquet of the wicked that dulls our appetite for heaven, but endless nibbling at the table of the world. It is not the X-rated video, but the prime-time dribble of triviality we drink in every night… The greatest adversary of love to God is not his enemies but his gifts. And the most deadly appetites are not for the poison of evil, but for the simple pleasures of earth. For when these replace an appetite for God himself, the idolatry is scarcely recognizable, and almost incurable."

For many of us, the great danger is not that we will renounce our faith. It is that we will become so distracted, rushed, and indebted that we settle for a mediocre, half-hearted version of Christianity. We have jobs, kids, and commitments. We have bills to pay, and relationships and reputations to uphold. Yes, we would love to experience a rich and satisfying relationship with God, but what choice do we have?

Learned Helplessness

Rejecting limits comes naturally—in fact, it was Adam and Eve's very first sin. According to the account in Genesis, Adam and Eve enjoyed fulfilling work without exhaustion, they experienced pure intimacy without any insecurity, and God had given them dominion over everything except the tree of the knowledge of good and evil. In other words, while living within the limits God had established, they experienced a deeply satisfying and uninhibited life. But Satan convinced them that God was holding out on them, and that they would become "like God" by rejecting His boundaries. So that's what they did, and that's what we do, too. But we were never supposed to be like God. Herein lies the problem. As technology progresses, we've come to believe that we can be like God: *all knowing* (omniscient), *everywhere at once* (omnipresent), and *all powerful* (omnipotent). One look at our calendars, bank accounts, screen time, and relationships reveals that we do in fact believe we can know it all, do it all, and solve every problem, everywhere, all the time.

We have become so accustomed to spending money, living a fast-paced life, and always being available through our phones that the thought of saying "no" or stepping away feels impossible. On those rare occasions we meet someone who doesn't own a smartphone or lacks a social media account, or someone who feels at peace being unavailable to people, we are suspicious, and maybe a little jealous. What if someone needs to get in touch with them? Aren't they being selfish? What about their children? Don't they get bored? Are we the crazy ones or are they?

We have developed what Martin Seligman and Steve Maier call "learned helplessness,"* accepting misery because we believe we have no other choice. But we do have a choice. I don't mean to imply that the choice is easy. Any time we walk into a store or restaurant, everything is designed to make it hard for us to say no. When we listen to a political advertisement or pundit, the objective is to make it unthinkable for us to vote for the other side. When someone texts and needs us to do something, it can feel rude to turn them down. By definition, choosing anything involves saying no to something else, or several somethings, and that can feel like a loss. But when we forget our ability to choose, we learn to be helpless. Drip by drip, we allow our power to be taken away until we end up becoming a function of other people's choices.

One of my favorite examples of embracing limits is about Napoleon. As a general, Napoleon made it a habit to delay responding to mail. His secretary was instructed to wait three weeks before opening any correspondence. When he finally did hear what was in a letter, Napoleon loved to note how many supposedly "important"

---

* Seligman and Maier divided German shepherds into three groups. The dogs in the first group were placed in a harness and administered an electric shock, but were given a lever they could press to stop the shock. The dogs in the second group were placed in an identical harness and were given the same lever, and the same shock, but the lever didn't work, rendering the dog powerless to stop the shock. The third group of dogs were placed in the harness and not given any shocks. Afterward, each dog was placed in a large box with a low divider across the center. One side of the box produced an electric shock, and the other didn't. The dogs that had been able to stop the shock and the dogs that had not been shocked at all in the earlier part of the experiment quickly learned to step over the divider to the side without shocks. But the dogs that had been powerless in the earlier part of the experiment did nothing to try to avoid getting shocked. Why? They didn't know they had any choice—they had learned helplessness.

issues had already resolved themselves and no longer required a reply. Even as I type that, I know it feels like quaint folklore that has no place in modern life. Napoleon didn't have email or Slack, and he wasn't in any group text threads. I told my doctor friend this story and he laughed and said, "Good for Napoleon, but if I don't respond, I don't get paid." My friend's not wrong. But isn't there some part of you that longs for that kind of control and courage—that kind of non-urgency to everyone else's demands of you?

A life without limits is a life without peace. It may not be obvious at first because of the emotional rewards our distractions give us, but as we've already learned, when unhealthy tendencies are normal, we don't recognize the damage they do to our interior life. But consider the way you feel when you have more commitments than time to dedicate to them. Consider how overwhelmed and anxious you feel when you have more financial obligations than money to meet them. Consider the stress you carry when you try to play savior for someone else's problems. We swear we just need a little more time, or a little more money, but we're lying to ourselves. What we need is the courage to say "no"—the audacity to embrace a life with limits.

Another Way

Christians have been experimenting with boundaries and limits since the beginning, seeking to find a way of life that keeps them aware of God's presence throughout the day. St. Benedict was the first to create a "rule" for this type of thing in his book, *The Rule of St. Benedict*, and it became the playbook for monastic life.

As a part of St. Benedict's rule, he instructed:

- Living in a monastery completely detached from the outside world
- Attending seven worship services a day, which included scripture reading, singing, and prayer
- Bible and scholastic study while outside of the worship services
- Manual labor to keep from getting bored or distracted

In very broad terms, this would be considered a monastic life. Whenever I teach about it, people get nervous, assuming this is what I'm going to ask them to do. Take a deep breath, no one is asking you to pray seven hours per day. But it's worth considering—if you had seven free hours available today, how many hours would you *want* to pray? If you could live in a monastery and rid yourself of a bank account or a calendar, would you want to? When we are disappointed with the quality of our spirituality, we fantasize about the perfect conditions for the Christian life—if we had a cabin in the woods, or less responsibilities. If we had more time, we would certainly be more spiritually minded. We imagine "utopias" free of inconvenience, neglecting the fact that our biggest barrier to experiencing God is not logistical, it's our longings. The thought of a life without the emotional rewards of distractions, busyness, or being needed forces us to confront our means of self worth. Much of our identity is tied to our income, zip code, how many things we accomplish, or how much influence we have. This is why you must acknowledge your deepest desires—because attaining what you want most usually requires you to go beyond God's limits for your life.

Embracing your limits means coming to terms with the fact that you cannot be everywhere, know everything, or fix everything. You cannot be who everyone else needs you to be and be who God wants you to be at the same time. You must make the choice to embrace your limits and let go of everyone else's expectations for you. This excruciating choice is perfectly explained in a fable from Edwin Friedman.

Once upon a time, there lived a man who had given a great deal of thought and effort to determine what he wanted from life. Then one day, a door opened for him to actually live his dream. But the opportunity would only be available for a short time, and he would have to embark on a long journey.

He began walking and grew more and more excited as he envisioned his future dream becoming a reality. As he hurried along, however, he came to a bridge high above a dangerous, rapidly-flowing river.

As he started across the bridge, he noticed a stranger approaching him from the opposite direction. The man had a rope wrapped many times around his waist. The rope looked like it might stretch to a length of at least thirty feet.

The stranger began to unwrap the rope as he walked. Just as the two men were about to meet, the stranger said, "Pardon me, sir, would you be so kind as to hold the end of this rope for me?"

Without thinking, almost instinctively, the man reached out and took the rope.

"Thank you," said the stranger. He then added, "Two hands now, and remember, hold tight."

Then the stranger jumped off the bridge!

The pull from the now-extended rope was so strong it almost dragged the man over the side of the bridge into the treacherous river below.

He shouted over the railing, "What are you trying to do?"

"Just hold tight," the stranger called back.

This is ridiculous, the man thought. He began trying to haul the stranger up, but the task was beyond his strength.

"Why did you do this?!" he yelled in frustration over the edge.

"Remember," said the stranger, "if you let go, I will die."

"But I cannot pull you up!" the man cried.

"I am your responsibility," said the stranger.

"I did not ask for it," the man said.

"If you let go, I am lost," repeated the stranger.

The man looked around for help, but no one was within sight.

He began to think about his predicament. Here he was, eagerly pursuing a unique opportunity to fulfill his dream, and now he was being sidetracked for who knows how long.

Maybe I can tie the rope somewhere, he thought. He examined the bridge carefully, but there was no way to get rid of his newfound burden.

Again he yelled over the edge, "What do you want?"

"Just your help," came the answer.

"How can I help? I cannot pull you in, and there is no place to tie the rope while I find someone else who could help you."

"Just keep hanging on," replied the dangling stranger. "My life is in your hands."

The man was stumped. *If I let go, I will always regret letting this stranger die. If I stay, I will never reach my dreams or destiny. Either way, this will haunt me forever.*

Time passed. Still no one came. The man became keenly aware that it was almost too late to resume his journey. If he didn't leave immediately, he wouldn't arrive in time.

Finally, a new idea came to him. "Listen," he explained to the man hanging below, "I think I know how to save you." He could not pull the stranger up solely by his own efforts, but if the stranger would shorten the rope by wrapping it around his waist again and again, together they could do it. But the dangling man had no interest.

"You mean you won't help?" he shouted to the stranger. "I can't hold on much longer!"

"If you don't, I will die," came the reply.

A revelation came to the man on the bridge—an idea that, until this moment, he would never have considered.

"Listen carefully," the man said. "I mean what I am about to say." The dangling stranger looked up, hopeless and despondent. "I will not accept the position of choice for your life, only for my own," the man said. "From this moment on, I give the power of choice for your own life back to you!"

"What do you mean?" the stranger asked, clearly afraid.

"I mean, simply, it's up to you. You decide your future. I will be the counterweight. You do the pulling and bring yourself up. I will tug some from here." The man unwound the rope from around his waist and braced himself to be a counterweight.

"You cannot mean what you say," the stranger shrieked. "You would not be so selfish. I am your responsibility. What could be so important that you'd let me die?!"

After a long silence, the man on the bridge said slowly, "I accept your choice." He let go of the rope and continued on his journey over the bridge.

We have all been the man on the bridge. We *are* the man on the bridge. Everyone needs something from us—our work, our friends, our children's hobbies, the list never ends. And when we do find a few moments of free time, our TVs and smartphones call to us, and we instinctively drown out the despair of boredom with more distractions and commitments.

In the next two chapters, we will look specifically at the limits of time and technology. But before we do, take a moment and imagine a life that isn't overcommitted, indebted, or distracted. Not an idealistic life living in the woods or on a beach, but a life in the exact same settings you currently live in, with a different set of values—a new way of life.

What is something you committed to that you wish you hadn't? What is something you financed that you wish you had declined? Is there someone else's problem you wish you could rid yourself of? Embracing your limits requires you to admit to yourself that you are limited, and that the life God wants for you is found outside of the overcommitted, overconnected life you're currently living. At first, as you begin to adopt a new way of life that creates margin and time for meditation, it will feel like you're being irresponsible, like you're letting others down or being selfish. But eventually, you will discover that you are living more like Jesus. More present, more personal, and more powerful. It's then that you will have the heart, soul, mind, and strength to love God and others the way you should.

Chapter Summary

» As you strive to *feel your feelings*, *face your past*, and *change your habits*, you'll need to embrace a new way of life—one that's less rushed, and more intentional.

» It's rarely the difference between obvious good and evil that causes us to miss real intimacy with God, it's just that we are too preoccupied. We are more busy than bad, more distracted than non-spiritual.

» When we are disappointed with the quality of our spirituality, we often fantasize about the perfect conditions for the Christian life—if we had a cabin in the woods, or less responsibilities. If we had more time, we would certainly be more spiritually minded, but our biggest barrier to experiencing God is not logistical, it's our longings.

» Embracing your limits means coming to terms with the fact that you cannot be everywhere, know everything, or fix everything. You cannot be who everyone else needs you to be and be who God wants you to be at the same time. You must make the choice to embrace your limits and let go of everyone else's expectations for you.

CHAPTER FOURTEEN

Striding or Striving?

> "The world is eaten up by boredom. To perceive this needs a little preliminary thought: you can't see it all at once. It is like dust. You go about and never notice, you breathe it in, you eat and drink it. It is sifted so fine, it doesn't even grit on your teeth. But stand still for an instant and there it is, coating your face and hands. To shake off this drizzle of ashes you must be forever on the go. And so people are always 'on the go.'"
> - **Georges Bernanos** *The Diary of the Country Priest*

In his book *Divine Mentor*, Wayne Cordero tells the story of a tree that was planted in 1606 in what would come to be known as Yosemite National Park. Eventually it would grow to be more than 240 feet tall, towering over the forest and becoming one of the titans of the park's redwood collection. But a few years ago, the tree fell. It was the first of Yosemite's Sequoias to fall in more than 100 years, so the forest service did an investigation to find out what had brought this massive tree down. There had been no windstorms, fires, floods, or lightning strikes, and no animal or insect damage, so what happened? As park rangers and forestry experts examined the downed behemoth, they came to a startling conclusion: *foot traffic*. They determined that the cumulative foot traffic around the base of the tree over the years had damaged the root system. So Yosemite decided to institute a policy of placing fences around some of the oldest trees "to keep the public from trampling the root systems of these giants."

In a way, embracing limits is like putting a fence around your soul to prevent everyone and everything else from damaging your root system. We know it's important. We can feel what the pace of our lives is doing to us. But time and time again, we find ourselves sacrificing our physical, mental, and emotional health for one more meeting, one more game, or one more task.

We are like Sisyphus, the Greek mythological figure who spent his life rolling a heavy stone to the top of a mountain, and each time he came agonizingly close to completing the task, the boulder would roll back to the bottom, and he would start again. This is 21st-century life. We convince ourselves that after a few more years of grinding or going or pushing through, eventually we will arrive at the destination we imagine in our minds, where we'll have what we want, and can live a different life than the one we're forced to live now. It's when the kids leave the house, or when we get the promotion, or when we get out of debt. We live with this agonizing fantasy that things will be better when we get "there," but we never seem to get there. The finish line always seems to inch further away.

In a letter to a friend, author Flannery O'Connor said, you have to "push as hard against the age that pushes against you." We would be wise to heed her warning, and as Christians, there is probably no area of life where we need to "push as hard as the age that pushes against us" than our pace of life.

In our culture, "slow" is how we describe things we're disappointed in. It's used in reference to bad service at restaurants, boring movies, and even people with lower IQs. The message is clear: slow is bad; fast is good. But spiritual depth is not a hundred-yard dash.

Remember, while deep change requires becoming more aware of your feelings, it cannot stay only in the emotional realm; it must be practiced in your day-to-day routines, responses, and reactions. It's easy to talk about spirituality in grand terms. We talk about God "changing our lives," and He can, but it's worth considering—has a relationship with Jesus even changed your schedule? We long for a transformational and transcendent experience with God, but we hope to squeeze it in between 7:30 and 7:45 a.m. on Tuesday. We want to know Him intimately, but we need Him to speak to us through one-verse inspirational devotionals. I'm not implying that any effort is wasted, but I am saying that we will never find the kind of deep connection with God we long for through social media slogans and motivational statements. Jesus taught that the Kingdom of God works like treasures that are hidden, like sheep that wander, bakers who mix yeast and dough, and seeds that are planted. This implies God's kingdom is experienced by people who have the *time* to search for treasures, walk with sheep, knead dough, and work the ground. There are no hacks or formulas. It isn't glamorous; in fact, it's painfully monotonous. But it is the pace of spiritual formation.

If we're not careful, we measure the effectiveness of our spirituality through the cultural standards of efficiency and productivity. We want to live a life that matters, but we measure ourselves by things that don't. Without hesitation, and mostly unknowingly, we embrace the ways and means of the culture as we go about our daily lives "in Jesus' name." But is that what Jesus would do? Is that how He would live?

Jesus Never Ran

It occurred to me recently that Jesus never ran. In the three years of His ministry captured in the four Gospels, there are no references to Jesus running. That's significant when you consider He only had three years to publicly teach, train 12 disciples, and meet all the needs of the people. Why walk when you can run? Why heal four people when you could heal five? Not only did Jesus choose not to run, when His best friends, Mary and Martha, implored Him to stop what He was doing because their brother Lazarus was sick, Jesus did not feel the need to change His plans or let someone else determine His pace. He stayed where He was for two more days, then finally, He decided to go visit them, after Lazarus had died.

Compare that to the way we respond to a text message or an email when someone needs something from us. Jesus' lack of insecurity and sense of purpose allowed Him to live with boundaries that very few of us can relate to. He knew who He was and why He was here, and for three years, He lived without the slightest hint of hurry.

This doesn't mean He had nothing to do. On the contrary, He

STRIDING OR STRIVING?

lived with an intense sense of mission and purpose. Of course, there is a healthy kind of activity where your life is full of things that matter, not wasted on empty pursuits. It's the difference between *striding* and *striving*. The word strive means to make a great effort to obtain or achieve something. Striving is not always a bad thing, but often it's why we put so much pressure on ourselves. We need to get more done in less time: make more money, commit to more activities, provide more opportunities for our kids. There is always more to obtain and achieve, and with just a little more effort, we can get it done. The word *stride*, though, means to walk with long, decisive steps in a specific direction. You're still living with purpose, and you can still improve, work, and commit to things, but you get to walk—you don't have to get it all done today, this week, or this year. Jesus lived with purpose, but He had nothing to prove, so for the three years of His public ministry, without the slightest hint of hurry, He took long, decisive steps toward the cross.

Over the years, after seasons of striving, I've had to admit to myself that most of my ambition and effort was an attempt to prove something or keep up with someone else. To be clear, wanting to accomplish something significant is not wrong, but feeling like it has to be done now, or feeling as if you're falling behind everyone else around you, is usually an indication you're trying to prove something. But let me remind you—you have nothing to prove.

In a letter to his son, a retired Eugene Peterson described the "blue funk" years, his early years in pastoring, as he struggled to find his identity.

"I think the first important thing that took place during those years was that I gave up thinking I was going to amount to anything. It took a while because I had always assumed that I would get to the top of something or the other... At the same time, I was sure I was where I was supposed to be... But I did have to reimagine my future in much more modest terms... I settled down to be a failure. I hoped that I could be a faithful failure..."

If you know anything about Eugene Peterson, you know that, of course, he was not a failure. He wrote 30 books, and single-handedly interpreted the Bible, giving the world *The Message* translation. His point was that he had to change his definition of success. The kind of life he needed to live in order to know God the way he desired would cause others to see him as a failure.

So why is it so hard? Shouldn't it be easy to embrace limits? Who wouldn't desire silence over the chaotic sounds of phones ringing or the TV droning? Who wouldn't desire a night at home, or a meal around the table, instead of more time in the car and more processed fast food and sugar? Who wouldn't want a good night's sleep over another episode of a show? Sadly, it's not as easy to embrace limits as it should be.

When I was a kid sitting in church, the preacher would talk about how we would never stop worshiping when we got to heaven, and it always disappointed me because all I could think about was how bored I would be, and how badly my feet would hurt having to stand that long. I wondered, "What are we going to *do* while we're there?" I've talked to enough Christians to know that it wasn't just me—sadly, the pace of life that Jesus modeled and described doesn't sound all that enjoyable, and the thought of heaven isn't as exciting as our plans for the upcoming holidays. The anxiety inside you that fears boredom reveals how your routines have trained you to need the adrenaline of busyness and created cravings in your life other than God's presence.

Rob Dreher calls this problem *everydayness*. This is how he described it: "Everydayness is my problem. It's easy to think about what you would do in wartime, or if a hurricane blows through, or if you spend a month in Paris, or if your guy wins the election, or if you won the lottery or bought that thing you really wanted. It's a lot more difficult to figure out how you're going to get through today without despair."

We've already learned about the emotional rewards of our routines and the need for spiritual disciplines, but it's worth revisiting as we consider our struggle to live within our limits—we are addicted to doing.

Doing Versus Being

It is significant that one of the first things Jesus did when He started His ministry was defy the need to prove His worth. When He was 12 years old, it was already obvious to anyone paying attention that He was not a normal child. His mom knew it, carefully watching and keeping all the prophecies and predictions about Him in her heart, but we don't hear anything about His life again until He's 30. In a culture where we rank the professional potential of 8th-grade basketball players, this seems odd to us.

18 years later, when Jesus was about to go public, something

significant happened. Before Jesus ever accomplished a single ministry assignment, He heard an affirming voice from His father that said, "This is my dearly loved Son, who brings me great joy." At 30 years old, the savior of the world had no public accomplishments. Still, God wanted Him to know that He was loved because of who He was, not what He did.

Sure of His father's love, Jesus was led into the wilderness for 40 days to be tempted by the devil, and it was there that His identity would be put to the test. With each temptation, Satan challenged Jesus' self-worth. The first two temptations focused specifically on *doing* as opposed to *being*—saying, in essence, "If you really are the Son of God, prove it."* The third temptation provided the opportunity to compromise and gain power without having to wait or suffer. But Jesus was able to resist each temptation because He felt no need to prove Himself—He knew He had nothing to prove.

Doing versus *being* is the first test Jesus had to pass, and it's one we have to pass too. As long as our insecurity drives us to prove something or gain someone's approval, we will rush to take on more than God calls us to, and slowly, over time, we'll forget that God loves us because of who we are, not who others think we are.

It was through receiving God's love, and getting away for 40 days of silence, solitude, and fasting, that Jesus was able to resist the temptation to prove His worth. We see again the power of spiritual disciplines and how they prepare us to make the right decision.

---

* The three things Satan tempted Jesus to do were turn stones into bread, jump off the temple, and bow down and worship him.

If our goal is to love God with all our heart, soul, mind, and strength, and to feel utterly loved and accepted by God, is there a way to live that would reinforce our desire for Him and make us feel more loved by Him? Yes! God has given us a way to stop proving our self-worth through our productivity and to get off the treadmill of the 21st-century grind.

Stop and Enjoy

When God was delivering His people from Egypt, He took them on a 40-year journey to teach them how to live in freedom. But after 400 years of ingrained slavery tendencies, like being defined by productivity, it was harder to live free than it was to live in slavery. So God gave them 600 laws to govern their way of life. He wanted a life of freedom for them, but this new way to live had to be learned, and the same is true for you and me.

While you may not be familiar with the 600 laws given to the Hebrew people, you're probably familiar with 10 of them, known as the Ten Commandments. These were the first 10 "rules" God gave Moses to teach the people how to live free. And while most people can recite a few of the commandments, like "thou shalt not kill, steal, or commit adultery," one commandment people typically forget is number five:

> "Remember to observe the Sabbath day by keeping it holy. You have six days each week for your ordinary work, but the seventh day is a Sabbath day of rest dedicated to the Lord your God."

In the list of 10 things God considered most important to teach His people a new way of life, He included the command to take a day of rest.

The word Sabbath comes from the Hebrew word *Shabbat*, and it can be translated as "to stop" or "to delight." So we could say that Sabbath is simply a day to stop working to enjoy God-ordained rest. Through Sabbath, you embrace your limits. "You let go of the illusion that you are indispensable to the running of the world. You recognize you will never finish all your goals and projects, and that God is on the throne, managing the universe quite well without your help."

This is a lot harder for us than it should be. It certainly doesn't come naturally. It's easier to keep going, keep working, and keep doing. As long as you are on the go, you can quiet the feelings of inadequacy and boost your self-worth by crossing more things off your list. But Jesus is inviting you to embrace a new way of life, a new pace, and a new definition of success.

Saint Augustine said, "You have made us for yourself, and our heart is restless until it rests in you." Sabbath is the primary practice that creates restfulness for your soul.

Ever since God gave His people the command to rest, they have been fighting and debating the intricacies and nuances of what exactly He meant by "rest." Ironically, the people who killed Jesus did so because they believed He was disobeying God's commands for Sabbath, but they were missing the whole point, like we so often do. We take something God meant to be beneficial and make it rigid and legalistic.

In our search for deep change, let's keep it simple and use three basic rules to help begin embracing limits and practicing Sabbath.

Rule #1: *Don't do things you normally do in your day-to-day life.* You're supposed to stop. So emails, task lists, meetings, chores, and errands are going to have to wait.

Rule #2: *Do something you enjoy.* The idea of sitting in a porch swing for a few hours may sound awful to you. Good news—you don't have to do something you hate. (Although it's worth considering whether you hate it because it forces you to feel helpless or worthless.) Choose things that are enjoyable to you.

Rule #3: *Make sure it's restful.* The whole point of Sabbath is to break away from the grind of accomplishing more. While you may enjoy landscaping, pulling weeds is not exactly a restful activity. Only you know your motives, so only you can decide if you are doing something because you enjoy it, or because it's something you need to mark off your to-do list.

As we end this chapter, take a few minutes and plan a Sabbath in the next seven days. Eventually you will want to create a predictable rhythm, but for now, just choose any day that works for you, and go ahead and make plans for what you will do, and more importantly, what you *won't* do. Remember, it's not just a day off. Typically, our days off are the days we do the things we didn't have time for on our days "on." No, Sabbath is a different way of thinking about life.

Walter Brueggemann said it best when he said, "People who keep Sabbath live all seven days differently."

As you practice Sabbath, you will become a different *kind* of person—a person more capable of loving God with all your heart, soul, mind, and strength. Not because you figured out how to squeeze it into your schedule, but instead because you decided to stop long enough to enjoy Him.

Chapter Summary

» If we're not careful, we measure the effectiveness of our spirituality through the cultural standards of efficiency and productivity. We want to live a life that matters, but we measure ourselves by things that don't.

» *Doing* versus *being* is the first test Jesus had to pass, and it's one we have to pass too. As long as our insecurity drives us to prove something or gain someone's approval, we will rush to take on more than God calls us to, and slowly, over time, we'll forget that God loves us because of who we are, not who others think we are.

» Sabbath is a day to stop working to enjoy God-ordained rest.

» **Rule #1:** *Don't do things you normally do in your day-to-day life.* You're supposed to stop. So emails, task lists, meetings, chores, and errands are going to have to wait.

» **Rule #2:** *Do something you enjoy.* You don't have to do something you hate. Choose things that are enjoyable to you.

» **Rule #3:** *Make sure it's restful.* The whole point of Sabbath is to break away from the grind of accomplishing more.

CHAPTER FIFTEEN

Easy Everywhere

"...how much happier that man is who believes his
native town to be the world..."
-Victor Frankenstein *Frankenstein*

Tell me if this sounds familiar. I grab my phone and swipe to the left twice. I click an app. I wait for the app to refresh. The pictures change. I scroll down. I scroll down some more. I've seen these before, so I scroll to the top of the app and pull down to refresh. The pictures change. But I've seen those too, so I exit the app and scroll right. I click to open another app. I scroll down, then scroll down some more. I'm uninterested, so I scroll to the top of the app and pull down to refresh. The screen changes. I'm done. I turn off the screen and place the phone on the table.

A few seconds later, I grab my phone. I swipe to the left twice, but I realize I just had this app open, so I scroll back to the right looking for an app I haven't opened recently. I find one. I open it. I scroll down. I scroll down some more. I realize I got distracted, so I turn off the screen and place the phone on the table. 90 seconds later, I grab my phone.

I think this is the point where I'm supposed to say, "Hi, my name is Jason, and I've been an addict for 15 years now," and you're supposed to say, "Hi, Jason."

Right now, as you read this book, you are facing a challenge that human beings have never faced before. You probably don't recognize it, because it feels as natural as breathing, but it's there tempting and taunting you every second of your day. What is the challenge? *Technology addiction*. Modern technology has harnessed the invisible, high-energy electromagnetic spectrum, so it literally is washing over you and coursing through your body every moment of the day—even while you sleep. It's those nervous twitches to check your phone or your watch just in case anyone is trying to reach you, or you received notifications from your bluetooth-connected video doorbell, washer and dryer, or robotic vacuum cleaner. Without your permission, technology—specifically the smartphone—has become the boss, dictating the terms, and we are servants obeying its every command. How did this happen?

First, let me define what I mean by technology. In modern terms, technology is a digital solution for a practical problem. There have been tools for as long as there have been human beings, but for most of history, those tools were quite limited. They weren't everywhere; they were in specific places. They remained in the field or in the kitchen or in the toolshed, and they helped people perform their work—they didn't work on their own. But modern technology hasn't simply made tools better or more efficient—it has given us completely new ways to get work done. More and more, the tools can perform the task for us. Author Andy Crouch calls technology "easy everywhere." It's having a profound effect on the way we live our life and interact with others, but more importantly, it's affecting the way we interact with God.

We all have some idea of the toll 24-hour connectivity is taking on our mental, physical, and emotional health, yet we can't embrace healthy technological limits in the way we know we should. I have never met anyone who regretted taking a break from their smartphone or social media, but somehow, like a mouse finding cheese, we end up trapped again. We instinctually grab our phones for those bright dings of pseudo-pleasure.

It's not an accident. We don't succumb to screens because we're lazy, but because billions of dollars have been invested to make this outcome inevitable. In a way, tech startups are the new tobacco farmers, and checking our "likes" has become the new smoking, and this all happened in about two generations.

It was January 2007 when Steve Jobs, then-CEO of Apple, made the groundbreaking announcement for the release of the first iPhone. I recently went back and watched his keynote address, and what shocked me was everything he *didn't* say the iPhone could or would eventually do. His vision was not constant connectivity to everyone and everything—his vision was an iPod that made phone calls. He spent the first eight minutes presenting its media features, concluding, "it's the best iPod we've ever made." Yes, they improved voicemail and touchscreens, but it's easy to forget that when the iPhone first launched, there was no app store, no social media notifications, and no front-facing camera, and all of these limitations were absolutely fine with its creator and the millions of people who purchased the product. That moment changed history forever, and there was no going back. The previous year, Facebook had opened up their platform to anybody with an email address, Twitter had launched its platform, and we had started using "the cloud" to collect and store our digital lives. We didn't know it then, but we were experiencing the start of the digital age.

The world has radically changed in a few short years, and not necessarily for the better. The Internet is decreasing our IQs, or at least our capacity to pay attention, it's dividing our country into polarized political silos, and it's increasing anxiety and depression, especially in teenage and adolescent girls. But you don't need to read the stats to know we're losing control. You can feel it when you have to slam on your brakes after getting distracted, when you accidentally ignore your kids trying to speak to you, and when you feel anxious that your phone's battery is running low or you don't know the Wi-Fi password.

Of course, no one signed up for this loss of control. We downloaded the apps and set up accounts for good reasons—we wanted to reconnect with high school friends, or see pictures of our nieces and nephews. But ironically, the tools designed to help us connect with our friends living hours away made us unable to connect with a friend sitting across the table from us.

My goal is not to be a naysayer, or deny the benefits of technology—I have as many devices in my home as the next person—but as we seek to have a deeply rewarding relationship with

Jesus, we must take an honest look at our limits, or lack thereof, with technology.

At its worst, technology fights against all the spiritual disciplines to some degree or another, but it is blatantly opposed to the spiritual disciplines of silence, solitude, frugality, secrecy, chastity, prayer, and fellowship. Of course, it can be used to enhance our spiritual experiences as well, but the creators of the devices and apps you are using are not ultimately concerned about your emotional health and spiritual depth. Their goal is to get your attention for as long as possible. You can see how this would be a problem for someone who desires to bear the fruit of the spirit. An honest evaluation would probably reveal that the constant stream of notifications has done very little to make us more loving, joyful, peaceful, patient, kind, or self-controlled.

So, is abstaining from all technology the answer? Not necessarily. As with the spiritual disciplines of abstinence, you may find that complete avoidance is needed for a predetermined period of time, but more likely, in order to coexist, you'll need to take some steps to put technology in its proper place.

Almost Amish

As you begin to consider embracing technological limits, you may experience a kind of fear, or skepticism that it's even possible. It feels like the whole world runs on our handheld devices, and if we decide to embrace counter-cultural methods, we wonder what we will miss or who we will disappoint. The thought of a less connected or less convenient life makes you feel like you're stepping back in time, but is that what we're trying to do? Are we trying to prevent progress or recapture an imaginary glory day of a "simpler time?" No, the goal is to limit what keeps us from becoming the *kind* of people we want to be—people who love God with all their heart, soul, mind, and strength.

A great model for us to consider is that of the Amish community. It's often incorrectly assumed that the Amish are frozen in time, reluctant to adopt any societal advancements after the eighteenth century, but that's not true—in fact, many Amish communities are pro-technology.

Kevin Kelly, who lived among the Amish and wrote the book, *What Technology Wants*, explains that the decision is left up to each individual community as to which technological advancements they will embrace and reject. The criteria they use to decide is based on one simple value: *Is this going to be helpful or detrimental for our community?* When a new technology is introduced, the leader of the community will grant permission for someone to try it out, then the community will observe the first adopter in order to try and discern the ultimate impact on the community's values. If the impact is deemed more negative than helpful, then it is prohibited. Otherwise, it is allowed, but usually with stipulations to maximize its positive effects and minimize its negative effects. This is why some Amish communities will use tractors, but only with metal wheels so they cannot drive on roads, or allow gas-powered wheat threshers, but require horses to pull machines. Personal phones are almost always prohibited, but a community phone booth is allowed.

My favorite thing about the Amish is the tradition of *Rumspringa*.

While they are very serious about their commitment to be "in the world but not of the world," they allow each member to make their own choice about belonging to the community. Beginning at age 16, Amish youth are allowed to leave home and experience the world beyond the restrictions of their community. After seeing and experiencing what they will have to give up in order to accept baptism into the Amish community, you might assume they would never want to return, but according to one sociologist's calculations, about 80–90 percent of Amish youth decide to stay after Rumspringa.[*]

The value-based decision model used by the Amish is a great model for us to consider as we seek to establish and embrace limits in our own lives and community. Are the tools that we use helping us become the *kind* of people we want to be? Usually, the answer is no. To the contrary, our devices are forming us into people we very much do not want to be. We are exhausted, always available, and never more than a text or email away. We are more insecure, constantly comparing our lives to the carefully-curated posts of our friends, and we are more addicted, spending as many as 9 hours each day consuming media.

Rates of teen depression and suicide have skyrocketed, much of which is seemingly due to a massive increase in anxiety disorders. Researchers found that the more someone used social media, the more likely they were to be lonely. Indeed, someone in the highest quartile of social media use was 3 times more likely to be lonely

---

[*] Of course, it's worth noting the power of tradition that influences us to stay in places more predictable and familiar to us. But the statistics are still staggering that given the choice between a modern life and a more "technology-free" life, overwhelmingly they choose to embrace the Amish way of life.

than someone in the lowest quartile. It turns out the technology that promised to connect us is making us feel more alone than ever before. But this probably isn't the first time you've heard alarming stats like these. So what do we do?

A Conscious Resistance

Technology isn't going anywhere—its reach and influence will continue to grow in society—but it's only good if it can help you become the person you were meant to be. So the question is, for a follower of Jesus who longs to love God and others with all your heart, soul, mind, and strength, what is its proper place?

There is no one-size-fits-all answer for that question; it will require wisdom for you to prayerfully consider the right solutions for you, and courage to do what you need to do. But as you consider the limits that are right for your situation, we can all use the same filter to decide what is best for us.

The Apostle Paul encouraged us to focus our thoughts on things that are "true, and honorable, and right, and pure, and lovely, and admirable"; things that are "excellent and worthy of praise."

As you consider your relationship with technology, would you say that it causes you to spend your time thinking about things that are true, right, lovely, and admirable? Or instead would you say that your current habits cause you to feel more fearful, overwhelmed, and insecure? With all the clickbait news headlines, videos, podcasts, endless photos, and constant commentary, we are consuming more than we were created to consume, and it's taking a toll on our nervous system. The only answer is some form of self-imposed limits—a conscious resistance to technology's default setting. I can't tell you exactly what they should be, but I will suggest three ideas to help you start defining your own limits.

Idea #1: Keep/charge your phone outside of your bedroom.

It may not sound like much, but not being able to instinctually grab your phone first thing when you wake up or last thing before you go to bed makes a difference. Plus, research has shown that being in the same room with your phone (even if it's turned off) makes you dumber—it reduces your "working memory and problem-solving skills." Not having your phone within reach can also help you establish firm starting and stopping times for use. Depending on your schedule, maybe you'll decide to leave your phone wherever it is until 10:00 a.m., or to put it away by 7:00 p.m., for example. Be warned, though—at first, that phone will be like a magnet pulling you back in. You will think of a hundred noble reasons why you need it by your side. But you don't. The world will go on, and your messages will be there when you get back to it.

Idea #2: Turn off your phone or keep it on "Do Not Disturb" for extended periods of time.

Maybe you want to turn off your phone completely as a part of your 24-hour Sabbath practice. If that's not possible, consider placing it in a mode that silences all rings, dings, and notifications. Andy Crouch adopted a "1 hour, 1 day, 1 week" principle for his family. The entire family turns off their devices for one hour in the evening for family dinner, one day a week for Sabbath, and one week a year for vacation. Maybe that would work for you.

I experienced one small example of this when returning from a sabbatical last year. While away, I rarely kept my phone with me, and came to enjoy the absence of the notification bells and dings that sound throughout the day. When I returned from my sabbatical, I made the decision to keep my phone in "silent" mode, so that I only picked it up when I wanted to, not as an instinctual response to a notification. 18 months later, I have still never turned on the sound. Yes, it causes me to miss a phone call every now and then, but the trade-off is well worth it.

Idea #3: Delete social media apps from your phone.

You may want to delete them for good, or you may want to just delete them for predetermined periods of time, but not having the apps on your phone will keep you from mindlessly scrolling. You can always log on through a browser or a computer if you need to access something. I've heard of people who ask their spouse or assistant to change their social media passwords on Monday morning and don't get the login access back until the weekend.

As with any temptation, hacks will only help so much. Eventually, you have to become the kind of person who isn't controlled by technology, but that doesn't mean you can't adopt a few principles to help make the effort easier. However you do it, it must be done. We will never be able to love God and others with all of our heart, soul, mind, and strength if we give our souls away to our devices.

So as you end this chapter, take a few minutes and consider your habits and your values. Do they align? Ask yourself these questions:

- What's the first thing you do when you wake up?
- How quickly do you consume news or media?
- What is your routine on the way to work?
- What do you do when you have nothing to do?
- What's the last thing you do before you go to sleep?

Think about all the devices you regularly use, or all the accounts you regularly sign into, and ask yourself: Does this device or app help or hurt my peace? Does it help or hurt my patience, my kindness, and my self-control? Depending on your answers, begin to establish limits for yourself and/or your family. Not because you have to, but because you want to be a different *kind* of person, and your current technological habits aren't helping you to do that.

Chapter Summary

» At its worst, technology fights against all the spiritual disciplines to some degree or another, but it is blatantly opposed to the spiritual disciplines of silence, solitude, frugality, secrecy, chastity, prayer, and fellowship.

» In order to coexist, you'll need to take some steps to put technology in its proper place.

» **Idea #1**: *Keep/charge your phone somewhere outside of your bedroom.* Not being able to instinctually grab your phone first thing when you wake up or last thing before you go to bed makes a difference.

» **Idea #2**: *Turn off your phone or keep it on "Do Not Disturb" for extended periods of time.* Maybe you want to turn off your phone completely as a part of your 24-hour Sabbath practice. If that's not possible, consider placing it in a mode that silences all rings, dings, and notifications.

» **Idea #3**: *Delete social media apps from your phone.* You may want to delete them for good, or you may want to just delete them for predetermined periods of time, but not having the apps on your phone will keep you from mindlessly scrolling.

EPILOGUE

Another Trip To Moriah

> "That is why the real problem of the Christian Life comes where people do not usually look for it. It comes the very moment you wake up each morning. All your wishes and hope for the day rush at you like wild animals and the first job each morning consists simply in shoving them all back; and listening to the other voice, taking that other point of view, letting that other larger, stronger, quieter life come flowing in. And so on, all day. Standing back from all your natural fussings and frettings; coming in out of the wind."
> -C. S. Lewis

My mentor is a man named Eugene Peterson, as you might guess from as many times as I've quoted him throughout this book. He didn't know it. We never met, and he died before I ever read anything he wrote. So I'm being a little presumptuous to call him my mentor, but I do it anyway. We spend most mornings together, me in my rocking chair in the corner of my room, and him sharing old transcripts of sermons he preached to his congregation in the '70s and '80s. He rarely gives me any advice. It's quite frustrating, really. He refuses to let me depersonalize God, to turn Him into slogans, lists, and helpful techniques. Come to think of it, he probably wouldn't like this book all that much, since it has diagrams in it. But his words and life have shaped me in profound ways, and he walked with me through the hardest and darkest season of my life.

A recurring topic in Eugene's work is the story of Abraham traveling to Mount Moriah to sacrifice what he loved most, his son Isaac. He writes about it in many of his books, constantly reminding me how the Christian journey—the life of faith—must be lived at Moriah. His point is that, as Christians, we need repeated reality checks. Our faith is never quite as strong as we assume, so we must be tested. And we cannot be trusted to test ourselves. "We are too full of self-interest and self-deceit. We are too devious at devising ways of cooking the books to document the evidence that serves our illusions."

As I thought about how to end this book, I kept coming back to Moriah.

A deeply rewarding and personal relationship with Jesus involves continuous adjustments—timely rescues from self-deceit. All along the way, we come to realize how our desires and attachments to this world cause us to domesticate God, and trivialize our faith until it helps us, but never inconveniences us. As Eugene would say, faith becomes a "wish upwards."

This is why, all along the way, God calls upon us to obey in some way that initially feels inconsiderate or inconvenient, but is necessary because sacrifice is the only way faith matures. "Only in the act of obedience do we realize the sacrifice is not diminishing. It does not result in less joy, less satisfaction, less fulfillment, but in more—but rarely in the ways we expect."

Somewhere along the way, you realize that you are no longer in charge of your life—that the life of faith does not consist of imposing your will. Instead, you begin the lifelong process of letting go of the idea that the world can function on your terms. Each surrender is a baptism of sorts—a cleansing of the residue of this world. You carry less. Life feels a little more "easy and light." A life of earning is gradually replaced by a life of receiving. And so, day after day, you return again to Moriah—the place of sacrifice.

To live by faith means to be tested. Untested faith does not yet qualify as faith. It's only after you lay down the thing you desperately want to cling to that you can be certain you have something more than wishful thinking. This almost always requires some form of pain. We can get very attached to this life, which we complain about, but love very much. It's only after we've relinquished it that we feel glad to be rid of it.

To find the life you desire, you must give up the one you're trying to manufacture—your deepest desires and beliefs. A life of faith requires a willingness to interrupt whatever you are doing and build an altar, to find whatever you happen to be carrying with you at the moment and place it on the altar, and to see what God wants to do with it. Initially we reluctantly oblige, wondering if it's worth it, but in time, like Jesus, we can say, "not my will but yours be done" and really mean it. For each Christian, this journey of faith—this invitation for deep change—begins the same way it did for Abraham, by simply telling God, "Here I am."

There's a sign that hangs in my barbershop that says: "Good, Fast, or Cheap: You can only choose two. Good and fast haircuts aren't cheap. Cheap and fast haircuts aren't good. Good and cheap haircuts aren't fast." The same is true for the Christian life. I didn't always believe that, but I do now. The seductive idea that drastic change happens in drastic moments has kept far too many Christians hopping around from church to church, or event to event, trying to capture some kind of transcendence in a bottle. They keep desperately hoping that a sermon, or a song, or a sign from heaven will magically change all the things they hate about themselves, and replace them with the character of Christ, but every experience falls just short of that glory day in their mind.

In stark contrast, Jesus said faith is like a mustard seed planted in a field. "It is the smallest of all seeds, but it grows into the largest of garden plants." It's not much in the beginning, but in time, it becomes something significant. Things like character and prayer cannot be mastered in quick ways, but speed is not the goal; transformation is. We want to be like Jesus not just in deed, but in essence—to love God with all our heart, soul, mind, and strength.

In one of Eugene's journal entries he wrote this:

> "All I want to do is become a saint—but secretly, so no one knows it—a saint without any trappings… every detail of routine and imagination, every letter I write, phone call made, gesture and encounter—gathered and placed on the altar and bound—every day another trek to Moriah."

You now have a better understanding of your instinctual habits and the influence of your interior life. You've learned the four practices that will help you experience a moment-by-moment relationship with the Holy Spirit. The opportunity for deep change is in front of you. You don't need to announce your intentions, or set deadlines for yourself. There's no point in looking for hacks or shortcuts. Instead, when you wake up tomorrow, just head to Mt. Moriah. Take all of your hopes and dreams—the way you think the world should work—and lay them down. I think you'll find that your life will feel more "easy and light" than it did before.

From the Author

Thank you for taking the time to read *Deep Change*. If you've made it to this point, you have made a substantial investment into your spiritual and emotional health. I truly believe that God is going to use the things you have learned and the practices you have started to bring about Deep Change in your life.

If this book has impacted your life positively I want to ask you to share it with someone you believe would benefit by reading it. As an independent author, word-of-mouth referrals are overwhelmingly the way the book lives on.

If you are a pastor or small group leader who would like to purchase bulk copies for your church or group, we would love to provide books as affordably as possible. Please email me at jason@realhopenow.com.

Acknowledgments

Thank you to the elders and congregation of Hope City Church, who have walked this Deep Change journey with me in large and small ways. It is a privilege to be your pastor.

Thank you to Katie, Kim, Jeremy, and Joe for reading hundreds of long text messages and giving me your feedback.

Thank you to Kristin for your exhaustive help, and for not letting me italicize *every* word.

Thank you to Andrea for letting me wonder and think out loud, and dominate the conversation while we drive.

Appendices

Appendix A

A Guide For Morning Reflection
(Visit deepchangebook.com to download a digital copy to use)

TAKE A FEW DEEP BREATHS AND A MOMENT OF SILENCE

"God, meet me now. In this stillness, quiet my heart so that I might try to earn nothing but instead only receive from You. Holy Spirit, help me be more aware of what is happening in my heart, mind, and body, and where I need to experience Your love and grace in my life today."

What am I angry about (feels unfair)?

What am I sad about (feels like a loss or shame)?

APPENDIX A

What am I anxious about (feels uncertain or nervous)?

What am I glad about (brings joy)?

What condemnation am I feeling about my sin/mistakes/failures/inadequacies? (Be specific about exactly what you're saying to yourself.)

Appendix B

An Explanation of Each Enneagram Type

Type One: The Perfectionist. Ethical, dedicated, and reliable, they are motivated by a desire to live the right way, improve the world, and avoid fault and blame.

Type Two: The Helper. Warm, caring, and giving, they are motivated by a need to be loved and needed, and to avoid acknowledging their own needs.

Type Three: The Performer. Success-oriented, image-conscious, and wired for productivity, they are motivated by a need to be (or appear to be) successful and to avoid failure.

Type Four: The Romantic. Creative, sensitive, and moody, they are motivated by a need to be understood, experience their oversized feelings, and avoid being ordinary.

Type Five: The Investigator. Analytical, detached, and private, they are motivated by a need to gain knowledge, conserve energy, and avoid relying on others.

APPENDIX B

Type Six: The Loyalist. Committed, practical, and witty, they are worst-case-scenario thinkers who are motivated by fear and the need for security.

Type Seven: The Enthusiast. Fun, spontaneous, and adventurous, they are motivated by a need to be happy, to plan stimulating experiences, and to avoid pain.

Type Eight: The Challenger. Commanding, intense, and confrontational, they are motivated by a need to be strong and avoid feeling weak or vulnerable.

Type Nine: The Peacemaker. Pleasant, laid back, and accommodating, they are motivated by a need to keep the peace, merge with others, and avoid conflict.

Explanations taken from Ian Morgan Cron and Suzanne Stabile, *The Road Back to You: An Enneagram Journey to Self-Discovery* (InterVarsity Press, 2016), 25.

Appendix C

Examples of Liturgies

For Drinking Morning Coffee/Tea

God, meet me this morning.

TAKE A FEW DEEP BREATHS AND A MOMENT OF SILENCE

In the stillness and quiet of the start of a new day,
Before the world needs something from me,
Before the sirens of worry,
   anxiety,
   and responsibility sound
Quiet my heart.

TAKE A FEW DEEP BREATHS AND A MOMENT OF SILENCE

There is no pressure today.
If I succeed or if I fail,
It doesn't change
   the way You see me,
   how much You love me,
   or why You saved me.

I need new mercies today:
  new peace from yesterday's conflicts
  new hope from yesterday's discouragements
  new strength from yesterday's works
  new faith from yesterday's doubts
  new love from yesterday's wounds

Let me be fully aware of my limits
  and Your grace at work in my life
I have nothing to earn, only everything to receive.

Amen.

For a Difficult Conversation or Confrontation

O Lord,
My heart is anxious.
I fear I will be misunderstood or hurtful
  to someone I love deeply.

Nevertheless, I know that this hard work
  is required for the greater good
  and the growth of all involved.

O Lord, when I am filled with assumptions,
  already certain of the truth,
  give me the wisdom and presence to be
  attentive, open, and fully present.

DEEP CHANGE

When needed, allow me to confront without attacking.
To question without accusation.
To defend without being defensive.

Help me to be courageous in the face of fear.
Don't let me cower from my responsibility
   to speak the truth in love.
Help me trust that Your greatest refining
   comes through painful truth that sets us free.

_____ is Your child,
  and You have entrusted me with
  the sacred, holy task of confronting them
  for their good.
Give me a father's heart.

Let the sting of accountability do its work.
Let there be more love, trust, and respect
   between us because we have done
   the hard work of caring for one another.
Help me to trust you are working toward Your greater purpose
   even in the midst of this conflict.

Amen.

APPENDIX C

For Feeling Like A Failure

I come to You, God, crushed by feelings of failure.
I have failed at my task,
   the people who depend on me,
   and Your calling on my life.

I struggle to believe that anything other than success or perfection
   could be pleasing to You, or good for Your kingdom.
How could these feelings of shame and confusion
   be for my good, or serve any greater purpose in my life?

Oh Lord, I have come to the end of my own strength,
   of trust in myself or my ability,
   which is where You desire me all along.

I need to be reminded again and again that,
   apart from the Spirit of God breathing life
   into my incomplete and sin-tainted efforts,
   apart from the Father blessing my inadequate offerings,
   apart from You Lord, meeting me and
   my stumbling attempts at faithfulness,
   no good work will come to fruition,
   no achievements will endure,
   no lasting benefit will come from my labor.

Let these feelings of failure drive me, oh Lord, to collapse on You.
Let me rest in the perfect work of Christ.

DEEP CHANGE

Let this fear do its work.
Let it be a messenger of grace, reminding me
   of what was true all along;
On my own, I do not have the strength, or the wisdom,
   or the ability to accomplish the task to which I am called.

Help me take heart, Oh God,
   that the outcomes of my efforts
   were never in my hands, but Yours.
You only ask that I be faithful.

God, Your thoughts are higher than my thoughts,
   Your ways higher than mine,
Who am I to judge the work of Your hands?
Is it possible that what I deem as failure
   will somehow be used for some greater purpose?

Use these feelings of failure, Oh Lord,
   to do in me what success and prosperity could never do.
Use them to make me more aware of
   my selfish ambitions and need for control.
Create in me a more humble and,
   sympathetic heart to the failings of others.
If this crash makes me more like You, Oh God,
   then even my greatest failures are a success in eternity.

So I relinquish now my agenda,

my need for control,
   and all my vain attempts to parse the mysteries of Your will

Use my dismay to place my confidence, again, only in You.

Amen.

For Feeling Disappointed or Defeated

God, I bring to You now the broken pieces of my expectations,
   hopes and dreams worn thin,
     my life as I once thought it would be.

What I wanted so badly has not come to pass.
My investment, passion, and
   effort only returned sorrow and frustration.
I know in my mind that You are sovereign,
   but in my heart I feel abandoned, confused, and disappointed,
   as if You do not care to let my hopes collapse.

Still, I know my heart is lying to me.
You are sovereign even of my sorrow.
You are always faithful,
   always lurking in the wings,
   always working,
     breathing on embers that seem like ash to me.

DEEP CHANGE

Looking back, I can see how what feels like neglect,
   is often new birth,
   a crucible burning away my lesser longing
   for something better, more eternal.

So let this disappointment do its work.

Let it tutor me.
Use it to unmask all of my false hopes.
Let me listen to its Holy whisper,
   that I might release lesser dreams
   and embrace better dreams You dream for me.
Teach me to place my hope always and only in You.

You are the king of my collapse.
You do not answer what I demand,
   but instead, what I do not even know to ask.

Now take this dream,
   this disappointment,
     remake it according to Your will or do not give it back at all.

Here in the ruins of my wrecked expectation,
I make this confession:

Not my will, oh Lord,
   not my dreams,
   but Yours be done.

Amen.

For Feeling Tired of Waiting on God

Read Psalm 25

Lord, I confess I do not understand Your timing.
If I were in charge of history and my life,
I would have arranged things differently.
I would not make me wait so long,
   or tease me with glimpses of good things to come.

You set my heart on things ahead,
   and fill my head with dreams
   but then leave them there,
   torturing me with moments of hope
   and seasons of discouragement
Why, God?

I feel exposed,
My impatience is revealing my sin and selfishness.
If I had everything I wanted,
I could hide in the comfort of certainty
But I would not need to trust You.

DEEP CHANGE

I cannot see the whole picture,
I cannot see from beginning to end,
   and so I wait for You.
TAKE A FEW DEEP BREATHS AND A MOMENT OF SILENCE

So God, here I am again,
Asking you to help me believe that:
   Your ways are higher than my ways
   Your thoughts higher than my thoughts
   Your timing is perfect
   and Your plans will never fail.

Be present in my waiting oh Lord.
Do not waste this discontentment,
Use it to reveal my unrighteous impatience,
   directed at circumstances and people.
Use these petty irritations and heartbreaking disappointments,
   to grow in me a greater longing for your return.

Amen.

Notes

Introduction-A Soul with Wings

1. "The box was broken for years... We called it 'making do.'": James Rebanks, *Pastoral Song: A Farmers Journey* (HarperCollins 2020), 45.
2. "Love the Lord God with all your heart, soul, mind, and strength.": See Deuteronomy 6:5
3. "like turning a horse into a winged creature": C. S. Lewis, *Mere Christianity* (C.S. Lewis Signature Classics, HarperCollins, 2009), 216. (Original work published 1952)
4. Do you feel that your old way of life has really "passed away?": See 2 Corinthians 5:17
5. "too trivial to be true.": Paul Scherer, quoted in Dallas Willard, *Spirit of the Disciplines* (HarperCollins, 1988), 24.
6. "How can ordinary human beings...follow and become like Jesus Christ?": Dallas Willard, *Spirit of the Disciplines: Understanding How God Changes Lives* (HarperCollins, 1988), 14.
7. "to write a great book, you must first become the book.": James Clear, *Atomic Habits* (Penguin Publishing Group, 2018), 8.
8. has very little effect on my feelings, habits, bodily tendencies, and social interactions.: Dallas Willard and Jan Johnson, *Renovation of the Heart in Daily Practice* (NavPress, 2006), 15.
9. "Come to me, all of you who are weary...": See Matthew 11:28-30

Chapter 1-Defining Normal

10. "I always believed any sin was easily rectified if only you let Jesus Christ into your heart, but here it gets complicated.": Barbara Kingsolver, *The Poisonwood Bible* (HarperCollins, 1998), 103
11. Our tendency is to either reduce Him to morals or platitudes...our lives remain unchanged.: Eugene H. Peterson, *As Kingfishers Catch Fire* (Waterbrook, 2017), 228.
12. "...it is not possible to be spiritually mature while remaining emotionally immature.": Peter Scazzero, *The Emotionally Healthy Leader: How Transforming Your Inner Life Will Deeply Transform Your*

Church, Team, and the World (Zondervan, 2015), 17.
13. **each time you repeat a behavior or a thought, you are reinforcing who you believe you are.**: James Clear, *Atomic Habits* (Penguin Publishing Group, 2018), 36–37.
14. **According to science, in a way, you can feel your thoughts.**: Derek Thompson, *Hit Makers: How to Succeed in an Age of Distraction*, (Penguin Books, 2017), 42–43.
15. **why the music you listened to as a kid always causes nostalgia**: New Music Discovery Stops at Age 33: https://www.wnycstudios.org/podcasts/takeaway/segments/music-discovery-stops-age-33-says-study
16. **"...but once you acknowledge your shadow...its power over you is diminished if not broken."**: Peter Scazzero, *The Emotionally Healthy Leader: How Transforming Your Inner Life Will Deeply Transform Your Church, Team, and the World* (Zondervan, 2015), 66.

Chapter 2-Why You Want What You Want

17. **"You will know the truth and the truth will set you free"**: See John 8:32
18. **science has proven that willpower is a commodity that eventually runs out.**: See the research from Roy F. Baumeister and John Tierney in their book *Willpower*. Several studies prove the same outcome—the quality of a person's choices decreases the more they are put in a position to have to make the right choice.
19. **accepting that he longed for intimacy, not simply sexual gratification, was transformational.**: David G. Benner, *The Gift of Being Yourself: The Sacred Call to Self-Discovery* (InterVarsity Press, 2015), 61–62.
20. **"...whatever is in your heart determines what you say."**: See Matthew 12:34
21. **you think as many as 6,200 thoughts per day!**: New study reveals just how many thoughts we have each day: https://www.newshub.co.nz/home/lifestyle/2020/07/new-study-reveals-just-how-many-thoughts-we-have-each-day.html
22. **Your thoughts are shaped by your emotions, and they are the last step before you act.**: For more information about the speed of your emotions versus logic (amygdala versus cortex) see a lecture by Glenn Veenstra Jr., PhD called, "Integrating Neuroscience and Family

Systems in Anxiety." You can find a similar reference (but with different response times) in *Childhood Disrupted*, page 124.
23. The Bible calls this "setting your mind.": See Colossians 3:2
24. why Jesus could compare anger and murder as equals.: See Matthew 12:34
25. "our own desires entice us, drag us away, and give birth to sinful actions.": My paraphrase of James 1:14-15

Chapter 3-Nothing to Prove

26. "Teacher, what good deed must I do to have eternal life?": See Matthew 19:16-22
27. There's another story Jesus tells in Luke about a father and two sons: See Luke 15:11-32
28. the way Eugene Peterson translated Jesus' instructions to pray: See Matthew 6:6 (MSG)
29. "Come to me... and I will give you rest.": See Matthew 11:28
30. Charles Spurgeon used to tell a story about a king who ruled over everything in a land: Charles Spurgeon's "The Carrot and The Horse": https://matthewzcapps.com/2014/03/31/charles-spurgeons-the-carrot-and-the-horse/

Chapter 4-Permission to Be Human

31. "find the door to your heart, you will discover it is the door to the kingdom of God.": Quoted by Peter Scazzero, *Emotionally Healthy Spirituality: It's Impossible to Be Spiritually Mature, While Remaining Emotionally Immature* (Zondervan, 2014), 80.
32. the pain of being human: Eugene H. Peterson, *As Kingfishers Catch Fire* (Waterbrook, 2017), 33.
33. keep adding fertilizer without admitting the existence of weeds and insects: My paraphrase of Eugene H. Peterson, *As Kingfishers Catch Fire* (Waterbrook, 2017), 46.
34. "You must bring him to a condition... clear to anyone who has ever lived in the same house with him or worked in the same office": C. S. Lewis, *The Screwtape Letters* (1996), 12. (Original work published 1942)

35. "The human heart is the most deceitful of all things, and desperately wicked.": See Jeremiah 17:9
36. he swore, "I would never!": See Matthew 21:33
37. They must pretend that they are strong and confident, not simply that they have strong and confident parts or that under certain circumstances they can be strong and confident. : David G. Benner, *The Gift of Being Yourself: The Sacred Call to Self-Discovery* (InterVarsity Press, 2015), 50.
38. 'what' questions…are better than 'why' questions: David G. Benner, *The Gift of Being Yourself: The Sacred Call to Self-Discovery* (InterVarsity Press, 2015), 43.
39. Consciousness of sin, inadequacy, and unworthiness is a regular part of worship.: Eugene H. Peterson, *As Kingfishers Catch Fire* (Waterbrook, 2017), 123.
40. "We cannot attain the presence of God…What's absent is awareness.": Richard Rohr, *Everything Belongs: The Gift of Contemplative Prayer* (Crossroad, 2015), 28.
41. Rich Mullins, the famous Christian singer…by the time he was in his forties it was about "four times a day: Tish Harrison Warren, *Liturgy of the Ordinary* (InterVarsity Press, 2016), 56–57.

Chapter 5-There's a Word for That

42. "Spiritual transformation does not result from fixing our problems… Turning to God in our sin and shame is the heart of spiritual transformation.": David G. Benner, *The Gift of Being Yourself* (The Spiritual Journey) (InterVarsity Press, 2015), 60.
43. Study after study reveals we are more lonely, depressed, anxious, and addicted than ever before: Megan Brennan "Americans' Mental Health Ratings Sink to New Low" https://news.gallup.com/poll/327311/americans-mental-health-ratings-sink-new-low.aspx
44. "Let all that I am praise the LORD; with my whole heart, I will praise his holy name.": See Psalm 103:1–2
45. we are "wonderfully complex.": See Psalm 139:14
46. On your piece of paper, write down four questions: I first heard this exercise in a seminar led by Peter Scazzero at Gordon Conwell

College called "Be Still and Know" on May 3, 2012.

Chapter 6-The Language of Prayer

47. prayer as a relationship with God "that becomes the context within which we experience all the events and relationships of our lives.": M. Robert Mulholland, *Invitation to a Journey* (InterVarsity Press, 2016), 127.
48. "pray without ceasing.": See 1 Thessalonians 5:17
49. "These moments are an opportunity for formation... And it exposes my idolatry of ease, my false hope in comfort and convenience…": Tish Harrison Warren, *Liturgy of the Ordinary* (InterVarsity Press, 2016), 54.
50. "worshiped the Lord at that place again.": See Genesis 13:4
51. "Our Father in heaven, hallowed be thy name.": See Matthew 6:9-13
52. "When your soul is spent... bigger than my own chaotic predicament and stronger than my own brittle resolve…": Pete Greig, *How to Pray: A Simple Guide for Normal People* (Navpress, 2019), 62–63.
53. a "prayerful imagination.": Eugene H. Peterson, *As Kingfishers Catch Fire* (Waterbrook, 2017), 60.
54. "…you pray high-mindedly for big but distant things... trace your distraction back to the real desires it comes from and pray about these.": Phillip Yancey, *Prayer: Does It Make Any Difference?* (Zondervan, 2006), 187.

Chapter 7-Looking Back to Move Forward

55. "The child is in me still… and sometimes not so still.": Ryan Holiday, *Stillness Is the Key* (Penguin Publishing Group, 2019), 105.
56. With the 72nd pick in the 1997 Major League Baseball draft: I first read about Rick Ankiel's story in *Stillness is the Key* by Ryan Holiday. This summary is based on Ryan's retelling, Rick's autobiography, and the article "Ankiel decides time is right to tell story of his battle with 'the monster'" by Derrick Goold in the St. Louis Post-Dispatch.
57. After the game, he swore... "It will never happen again.": Letter to My Younger Self: https://www.theplayerstribune.com/articles/rick-ankiel-letter-to-my-younger-self-cardinals

58. "Because otherwise why would he say that stuff to me? Why would he be so angry?": Rick Ankiel, *The Phenomenon* (PublicAffairs, 2017), 106.
59. "The fights of my childhood... the villain was within me, restless and relentless and just out of reach.": Rick Ankiel, *The Phenomenon* (PublicAffairs, 2017), 6.
60. "One moment, I was a pitcher.... I was, quite suddenly, my father's son.": Rick Ankiel, *The Phenomenon* (PublicAffairs, 2017), 107.
61. I read recently about the Europa, a hotel in Ireland that earned the nickname, "the most bombed hotel in the world.": Life goes on at the most bombed hotel in the world: https://www.irishtimes.com/life-and-style/people/life-goes-on-at-the-most-bombed-hotel-in-the-world-1.2901861
62. That is the promise of God in Jesus Christ and the experience that is at the heart of Christian living—conversion.: Eugene H. Peterson, *On Living Well: Brief Reflection on Wisdom for Walking in the Way of Jesus* (Waterbrook, 2021), 5.

Chapter 8-Family of Origin

63. 'Sometimes father and I were living together...it seemed as natural as the variations of the weather and the seasons.": Thomas Merton, *The Seven Storey Mountain: An Autobiography of Faith* (Harcourt Inc., 1948), 20–21.
64. To help understand duration neglect, let's use a hypothetical family vacation to Disney World: Hypothetical example taken from Chip and Dan Heath, *The Power of Moments* (Simon & Schuster, 2017), 6-9.
65. "...for I, the LORD your God, am a jealous God, punishing the children for the sin of the fathers to the third and fourth generations...": See Exodus 20:4–6
66. In the same way, we may leave home, but we continue to unconsciously follow the "rules" we internalized in our families of origin.: Peter Scazzero, *Emotionally Healthy Spirituality: It's Impossible to Be Spiritually Mature, While Remaining Emotionally Immature* (Zondervan, 2014), 100.
67. "a baby takes that as a signal that the mother desires the object, or is at least paying attention to it because it must be important.": Luke

Burgis, *Wanting: The Power of Mimetic Desire In Everyday Life* (St. Martin's Press, 2021), 25–26.
68. **And it is often the case... rather than a reflection on us or their love for us.**: Peter Scazzero, *Emotionally Healthy Spirituality: It's Impossible to Be Spiritually Mature, While Remaining Emotionally Immature* (Zondervan, 2014), 109.
69. **Abraham was an incredible example of faith, but under pressure, he reverted to being dishonest.**: See Genesis 20
70. **David's kids also lived with intense feelings of rivalry, including murder, sexual abuse, and one of the sons trying to kill his dad.**: See 2 Samuel 15–19
71. **Find mor about the "10 Family Commandments" in:** Peter Scazzero, *Emotionally Healthy Spirituality: It's Impossible to Be Spiritually Mature, While Remaining Emotionally Immature* (Zondervan, 2014), 99.

Chapter 9-The Story of Pain

72. **"How shalt thou hope for mercy, rendering none?"**: Shakespeare, *Merchant of Venice*, 4.1.88
73. **"Of the Seven Deadly Sins, anger is possibly the most fun... The skeleton at the feast is you."**: Frederick Buechner, *Wishful Thinking: A Theological ABC* (New York: Harper & Row, 1973), 2.
74. **St. Augustine's argument that envy and hatred try to pierce our neighbor with a sword, when the blade cannot reach him unless it first passes through our own body:** taken from Thomas Merton, *The Seven Storey Mountain: An Autobiography of Faith* (Harcourt, 1948), 60.
75. **Jesus instructed his disciples to halt worship in pursuit of reconciliation:** See Matthew 5:23–24
76. **Myth becomes myth in the retelling:** Paraphrase of a quote from David Maraniss in *Ego is the Enemy* by Ryan Holiday, pg. 107
77. **Story about Rebecca taken from:** Philip Yancey, *What's So Amazing About Grace?* (Zondervan, 1997), 105–106.
78. **you can contrive a hundred reasons against forgiveness:** Examples taken from Philip Yancey, *What's So Amazing About Grace?* (Zondervan, 1997), 96.

79. "Forgive us our trespasses as we forgive those who trespass against us.": See Matthew 6:12–14
80. "Father, forgive them, for they don't know what they are doing.": See Luke 23:34
81. you are the person Jesus described, who has been forgiven of a debt far greater than you are owed: See Matthew 18:21–35

Chapter 10-The Overstimulated Soul

82. "The soul that rises from sin to devotion may be compared to the dawning of the day... little by little.": Francis de Sales, *Introduction to the Devout Life*, trans. John K. Ryan (Garden City, NY: Doubleday, Image Books, 1957), 43–44.
83. Researchers at Columbia University wanted to better understand first impressions: Malcolm Gladwell, *Blink: The Power of Thinking Without Thinking* (First Back Bay, 2007), 61–65.
84. "I want to do what is good, but I don't. I don't want to do what is wrong, but I do it anyway.": See Romans 7:19
85. "the spirit is willing but the body is weak.": See Matthew 26:41
86. the part of your brain responsible for seeking pleasure quickly makes a switch... when you anticipate it.: Addicted to Anticipation: What goes wrong in the brain chemistry of a gambling addict: https://medium.com/s/nautilus-learning/addicted-to-anticipation-fe8ef573f326
87. "there is another power within me that is at war with my mind. This power makes me a slave to the sin that is still within me.": See Romans 7:22–23
88. When humans rescue baby animals in the wild, the animals are said to be "imprinted,": See this idea in Tish Harrison Warren, *Liturgy of the Ordinary* (InterVarsity Press, 2016), 26–27.
89. "I was the slave, not the master, of an impulse, which I detested, yet could not disobey ... an element which I had willingly chosen.": Mary Shelley, *Frankenstein*, (Penguin Classics, 1992), 219. (Original work published 1818)
90. "Thank heaven, I have given up smoking again! God! I feel it. Homicidal, but fit. A different man. Irritable, moody, depressed, rude, nervy, perhaps; but the lungs are fine.": Quoted in *Willpower: Rediscovering the Greatest Human Strength* by Roy F. Baumeister and

John Tierney. (Penguin, 2011), 31.

Chapter 11-Spiritual Disciplines

91. "After the first few steps in the Christian life we realise that everything which really needs to be done in our souls can be done only by God.": C. S. Lewis, *Mere Christianity* (C. S. Lewis Signature Classics, HarperOne, 2009), 193. (Original work published 1952)
92. It is more like painting a portrait than like obeying a set of rules.... He is beginning, so to speak, to 'inject' His kind of life and thought, His Zoe, into you...": C.S. Lewis, *Mere Christianity* (C. S. Lewis Signature Classics, HarperOne, 2009), 189. (Original work published 1952)
93. "If we feel that any habit or pursuit, harmless in itself, is keeping us from God... it is necessary that we should steadily resolve to give up anything that comes between ourselves and God.": William Ralph Inge, *Goodness and Truth* (London: Mowbray, 1958), 76–77.
94. the kind of role-playing Jesus warned his disciples about: See Matthew 6:6 MSG Translation
95. "as often times as I was among men I came back a less man, that is to say less holy.": Thomas à Kempis, Irwin Edman, ed., *The Imitation of Christ, in The Consolations of Philosophy* (New York: Random House, Modern Library, 1943), 153–55.
96. "people who love one another can be silent together.": Eberhard Arnold, "*Why We Choose Silence Over Dialogue,*" *The Plough, a publication of the Bruderhof communities*, no. 11, (July/August 1985): 12.
97. Jesus told the disciples that it is possible to fast and not appear to others as if you feel miserable.: See Matthew 6:16–18
98. "when so many people seem to wish to be great in God's eyes, there are so few who are truly saintly. 'The chief reason,' he replied, 'is that they give too big a place in life to indifferent things.'": Quoted in William R. Parker and Elaine St. Johns, *Prayer Can Change Your Life* (Carmel, NY: Guideposts Associates, 1957), 40.
99. "what is better.": a reference to Jesus' comments to Martha in Luke 10:42
100. Jesus taught his disciples that it is possible to willingly sacrifice sexual pleasure for the Kingdom of God.: See Matthew 19:11–12

NOTES

101. "the essence of chastity is not the suppression of lust but the total orientation of one's life toward a goal.": Dietrich Bonhoeffer, *Letters and Papers from Prison* (London: Fontana, 1953), 163.
102. In time, we "learn to love to be unknown and even to accept misunderstanding without the loss of our peace, joy, or purpose,": Dallas Willard, *The Spirit of the Disciplines* (HarperCollins, 1988), 172–173.
103. "the cautious faith that never saws off the limb on which it is sitting never learns that unattached limbs may find strange, unaccountable ways of not falling.": Dallas Willard, *The Spirit of the Disciplines* (HarperCollins, 1988), 175.
104. the time Jesus healed the lame man and commanded him to "take up [his] mat and walk,": See John 5:8
105. Jesus said that someone who builds their life on His words ... someone who doesn't is like living in a house that crumbles every time a storm comes.: See Matthew 7:24–27
106. "Mystics without study are only spiritual romantics who want relationship without effort.": Calvin Miller, *The Table of Inwardness* (Downers Grove, IL: Inter-Varsity Press, 1984), 83.
107. "we dishonor God as much by fearing and avoiding pleasure as we do by dependence upon it or living for it.": Dallas Willard, *The Spirit of the Disciplines* (HarperCollins, 1988), 180.
108. Jesus instructed his disciples to try to be alone in a quiet place, and let go of the pressure to use a lot of words: See Matthew 6:5–7
109. there is the potential for power that is different when practiced alone.: See Matthew 18:19–20 or James 5:14, for example
110. Confession removes the psychological and physical burden that comes from hidden sin: See Psalm 32:3
111. "though He was God, did not think of equality with God as something to cling to. Instead, He gave up His divine privileges; and took the humble position of a servant.": My paraphrase of Phillippians 2:6–7
112. $3 Worth of God Poem: Wilbur E. Rees, *$3.00 Worth of God* (Valley Forge [Pa.]: Judson Press, 1971).

Chapter 12-Something More Beautiful

113. "I can resist everything except temptation.": Quoted in *Willpower*:

Rediscovering the Greatest Human Strength by Roy F. Baumeister and John Tierney. (Penguin 2011) 5

114. "the sweetness of sanctified living.": A Devotional Reading: Odysseus (Escape) or Jason (Delight)?: https://asburyseminary.edu/elink/devotional-reading-odysseus-escape-jason-delight/
115. Think of it as a "saint" and "sinner" version of yourself.: Concept taken from an Instagram post by Peter Scazzero: https://www.instagram.com/p/Ca5OJv-hdEg/
116. "Good and evil both increase at compound interest… from which the enemy may launch an attack otherwise impossible.": C. S. Lewis, *Mere Christianity* (C. S. Lewis Signature Classics, HarperOne, 2009), 132. (Original work published 1952)
117. Study after study has found that people with more supposed willpower are really just people who rarely need to use it because they do not position themselves in situations requiring hard choices.: For more information about the myths about willpower see the findings by Roy F. Baumesiter and John Tierney in their book *Willpower: Rediscovering the Greatest Human Strength*.

Chapter 13-The Courage To Say No

118. "In proportion as our inward life fails… has not heard from himself this long while.": Henry David Thoureau, "Life Without Principle," The Atlantic Monthly, October 1863, https://www.theatlantic.com/magazine/archive/1863/10/life-without-principle/542217/.
119. whenever we are unsure how to act, we look to the majority to guide our behavior.: James Clear, *Atomic Habits* (Penguin Publishing Group, 2018), 118–119.
120. only 2.5% of people are innovators, and only 13.5% are early adopters.: See The Rogers Adoption Curve & How You Spread New Ideas Throughout Culture: https://medium.com/the-political-informer/the-rogers-adoption-curve-how-you-spread-new-ideas-throughout-culture-d848462fcd24
121. 18% of Americans use a mood-altering substance nearly every day: See Mood-Altering Drug Use Highest in West Virginia, Lowest in Alaska from Gallup: https://news.gallup.com/poll/182192/mood-altering-drug-highest-west-virginia-lowest-alaska.aspx#:~:text=Nationally%2C%2018.9%25%20of%20Americans%20

report,or%20medication%20rarely%20or%20sometimes.
122. **40 million people a year experience an impairment because of an anxiety disorder:** Anxiety disorders are the most common mental illness in the U.S., affecting 40 million adults, or 18.1% of the population, every year. See Facts & Statistics from the ADAA: https://adaa.org/understanding-anxiety/facts-statistics
123. **39% of Americans reported being more anxious than they were a year ago.:** See Americans Say They are More Anxious; Baby Boomers Report Greatest Increase in Anxiety from the APA: https://www.psychiatry.org/newsroom/news-releases/americans-say-they-are-more-anxious-than-a-year-ago-baby-boomers-report-greatest-increase-in-anxiety
124. **We are like the people Jesus described in the parable of the great feast... they have too many other seemingly noble obligations:** See Luke 14:16–20
125. **"The greatest enemy of hunger for God is not poison but apple pie... For when these replace an appetite for God himself, the idolatry is scarcely recognizable, and almost incurable.":** John Piper, *A Hunger for God: Desiring God through Fasting and Prayer* (Good News Publishers, 1997) 18.
126. **For more information about "Learned Helplessness":** See pg. 36 of *Essentialism* by Greg McKeown (The Crown Publishing Group, 2014).
127. **Drip by drip, we allow our power to be taken away until we end up becoming a function of other people's choices.:** Greg McKeown, *Essentialism* (The Crown Publishing Group, 2014), 40.
128. **Napoleon loved to note how many supposedly "important" issues had already resolved themselves and no longer required a reply.:** Ryan Holiday, *Stillness Is the Key* (Penguin Publishing Group, 2019), 30.
129. **Man on the bridge fable:** I read this fable in *Emotionally Healthy Discipleship* by Peter Scazzero, but it is an adaptation originally found in *Friedman's Fables*. Edwin H. Friedman, (New York: Guilford Press, 1990), 9–13.

Chapter 14-Striving or Striding?

130. **"The world is eaten up by boredom...And so people are always 'on the go.'":** Georges Bernanos, *The Diary of a Country Priest* (Da Capo

Press, 2002), 2.
131. Story about tree falling in Yosemite: Wayne Cordeiro, *The Divine Mentor: Growing Your Faith as You Sit at the Feet of the Savior* (Baker Publishing Group, 2007), 15–16.
132. "push as hard against the age that pushes against you.": Flannery O'Connor, *The Habit of Being: Letters of Flannery O'Connor*, ed. Sally Fitzgerald (New York: Farrar, Straus and Giroux, 1979), 229.
133. In our culture, "slow" is how we describe things we're disappointed in... The message is clear: slow is bad; fast is good: Paraphrase of John Mark Comer, *The Ruthless Elimination of Hurry* (The Crown Publishing Group, 2019), 24.
134. "I think the first important thing that took place during those years was that I gave up thinking I was going to amount to anything... I hoped that I could be a faithful failure...": Eugene Peterson and Eric Peterson, *Letters to a Young Pastor: Timothy Conversations Between a Father and Son* (Navpress, 2020), 41.
135. "Everydayness is my problem... It's a lot more difficult to figure out how you're going to get through today without despair.": Rod Dreher, "Everydayness," The American Conservative (blog), November 12, 2012, www.theamericanconservative.com/dreher/everydayness-wallace-stevens.
136. "This is my dearly loved Son, who brings me great joy.": See Matthew 3:17
137. "Remember to observe the Sabbath day by keeping it holy. You have six days each week for your ordinary work, but the seventh day is a Sabbath day of rest dedicated to the Lord your God.": See Exodus 20:8
138. Through Sabbath, you embrace your limits... God is on the throne, managing the universe quite well without your help.: Peter Scazzero, *The Emotionally Healthy Leader: How Transforming Your Inner Life Will Deeply Transform Your Church, Team, and the World* (Zondervan, 2015), 147.
139. "You have made us for yourself, and our heart is restless until it rests in you.": Saint Augustine of Hippo, *The Confessions of Saint Augustine* (New York: Doubleday, 1960), 43.
140. "People who keep Sabbath live all seven days differently.": Walter Brueggemann, *Sabbath as Resistance: Saying No to the Culture of Now* (Louisville, KY: Westminster John Knox Press, 2014), 67.

NOTES

Chapter 15-Easy Everywhere

141. "how much happier that man is who believes his native town to be the world…": Mary Shelley, *Frankenstein*, (Penguin Classics, 1992), 43. (Original work published 1818)
142. Andy Crouch calls technology "easy everywhere.": Andy Crouch, *The Tech-Wise Family: Everyday Steps for Putting Technology in Its Proper Place* (Baker Books, 2017), 51.
143. those bright dings of pseudo-pleasure.: Paul Lewis, "'Our minds can be hijacked': the tech insiders who fear a smartphone dystopia," Guardian, October 6th, 2017. https://www.theguardian.com/technology/2017/oct/05/smartphone-addiction-silicon-valley-dystopia
144. We don't succumb to screens because we're lazy, but because billions of dollars have been invested to make this outcome inevitable.: Cal Newport, *Digital Minimalism: Choosing a Focused Life In A Noisy World* (Portfolio/Penguin, 2019), 9.
145. tech startups are the new tobacco farmers, and checking our "likes" has become the new smoking: "Social Media is the New Nicotine." Real Time with Bill Maher. HBO. May 12, 2017.
146. Is this going to be helpful or detrimental for our community?: My paraphrase of Jeff Brady, "Amish Community Not Anti-Technology, Just More Thoughtful," All Things Considered, NPR, September 2, 2013, https://www.npr.org/sections/alltechconsidered/2013/09/02/217287028/amish-community-not-anti-technology-just-more-thoughtful
147. Statistics about smartphone usage, rates of teen depression, and the correlation between usage and lonliness: taken from Cal Newport, *Digital Minimalism: Choosing a Focused Life in a Noisy World* (Portfolio/Penguin, 2019), 104, 106, 139.
148. things that are "true, and honorable, and right, and pure, and lovely, and admirable;" things that are "excellent and worthy of praise.": See Phillippians 4:8
149. being in the same room with your phone makes you dumber: Robinson Meyer, "Your Smartphone Reduces Your Brainpower, Even If It's Just Sitting There: A Silent, Powered-Off Phone Can Still Distract the Most Dependent Users," Atlantic, August 2, 2017, www.theatlantic.com/technology/archive/2017/08/a-sitting-phone-gathers-brain-dross/535476.

Epilogue-Another Trip To Moriah

150. "We are too full of self-interest and self-deceit. We are too devious at devising ways of cooking the books to document the evidence that serves our illusions.": Eugene H. Peterson, *The Jesus Way: A Conversation on the Ways That Jesus Is the Way* (Eerdmans, 2007), 53.
151. a "wish upwards.": Eugene H. Peterson, *The Jesus Way: A Conversation on the Ways That Jesus is the Way* (Eerdmans, 2007), 49.
152. "Only in the act of obedience do we realize the sacrifice is not diminishing. It does not result in less joy, less satisfaction, less fulfillment, but in more—but rarely in the ways we expect.": Eugene H. Peterson, *The Jesus Way: A Conversation on the Ways That Jesus Is the Way* (Eerdmans, 2007), 51
153. "It is the smallest of all seeds, but it grows into the largest of garden plants.": My paraphrase of Matthew 13:31-32
154. "All I want to do is become a saint—but secretly, so no one knows it...every day another trek to Moriah.": Winn Collier, *A Burning In My Bones: The Authorized Autobiography of Eugene H. Peterson* (Waterbrook, 2021), 223.